THE LITTLE HISTORY OF SCOTTISH BREWING

JOHN ALEXANDER

First published 2022

The History Press
97 St George's Place, Cheltenham,
Gloucestershire, GL50 3QB
www.thehistorypress.co.uk

British Library Cataloguing in Publication Data.
A catalogue record for this book is available from the British Library.

ISBN 978 1 80399 108 5

Typesetting and origination by The History Press
Printed and bound in Great Britain by TJ Books Limited, Padstow, Cornwall

CONTENTS

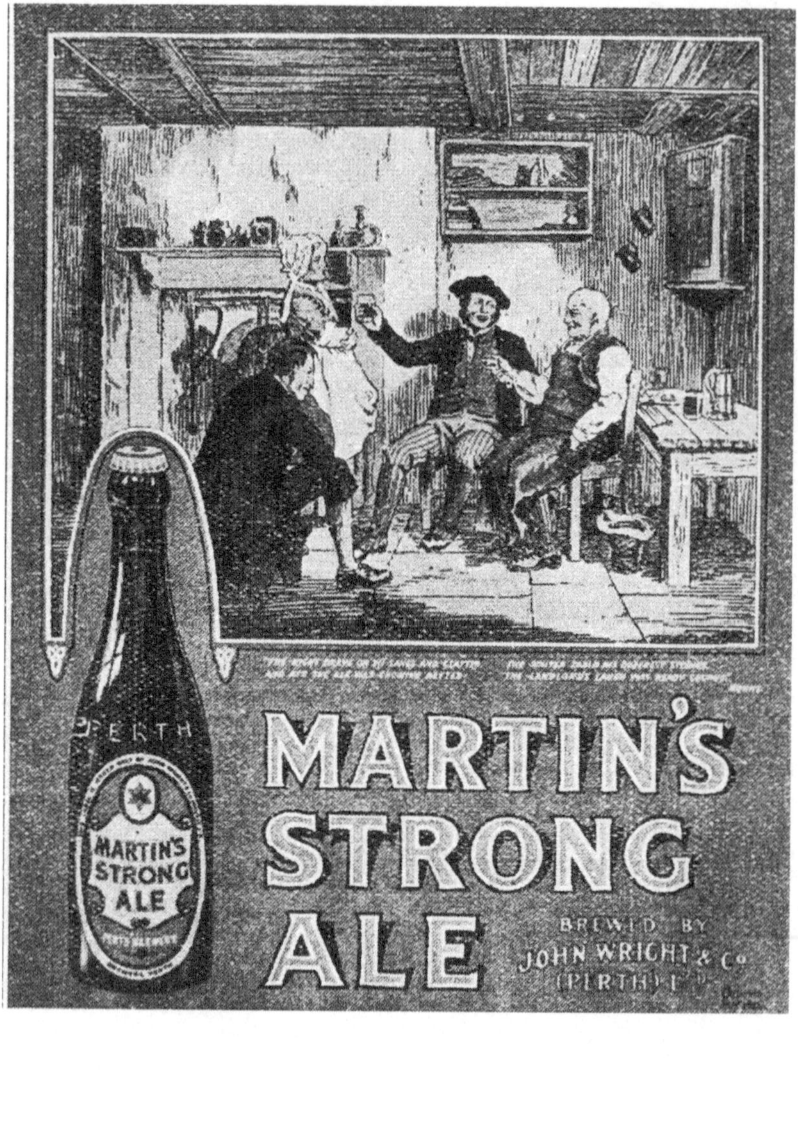

MARTIN'S
STRONG
ALE

BREWED BY
JOHN WRIGHT & Co
(PERTH) LTD

ACKNOWLEDGEMENTS

Much of the following story has been collated over many years and the following people have all contributed in some way to the success of this book. Thanks to Innes Duffus, archivist of the Nine Incorporated Trades of Dundee. Iain McInally, Dr Les. Howarth, Kenny Mowbray and the late Bill Cooper of Scottish Craft Brewers. Keith Robson DA. The late Sandy Hunter, Monkscroft, Belhaven Brewery, Dunbar. Stuart Cail, Head Brewer, Harviestoun Brewery, Alloa. The late Gilbert Dallas, MBE, Dougall McCrorie, founder of the Craft Brewing Association. Paul Taylor, Laboratory Manager at Murphy's, Nottingham. Duncan McAra, Scottish Tall Fount Supporters. Eric Dore of the Labologist's Society. The late Dr David Johnston, ex-Head Brewer at Tennent's, Glasgow. The late Harvey Milne, former brewer with Arrol's Alloa Brewery. Simon MacMillan, BA Hons. CAMRA members Forbes Brown and Dr Stuart Rivers. Charles McMaster, BA, former archivist at the Scottish Brewing Archive, Edinburgh. Also, to Alma Topen, who became the archivist at the Scottish Brewing Archive, Glasgow University, at a very difficult time in 1992. To Sandra Gordon, researcher at the James Hutton Institute, Invergowrie and Howard Davis, ex-Director of the James Hutton Institute, Invergowrie, Perthshire.

INTRODUCTION

Brewing developed throughout the British Isles over a long period of time by practical and empirical processes, from simple cottage, farm and tavern brewing to eventual commercial brewing. Brewing was like baking, a local industry and commerce that was limited to how far a horse could travel in one day. In Scotland, the Browster-wives were the mainstay of domestic brewing scene and were numerous in every town and locality, and excess production was sold to the community. The Luckies brewed in the ale houses and were the forerunners of large-scale commercial brewing.

Most of the early beers, brewed with groot in Scotland, were sorry stuff, and it was only in the early 1700s that things started to change with the introduction of the hop, which had a huge impact on Scottish brewing, alongside improvements in agriculture that took place during the Industrial Revolution, plus the growth of the wage economy that saw a brewing industry develop in Scotland that was second to none.

There is nothing nationalistic about my history; it is just that I believe Scotland has a story to be told and no claim is made that we did it alone as, historically, brewers throughout Europe in some way exchanged information on their ingredients and methods. The creation of London Porter in the early 1700s also had a huge influence on fortunes of Scottish brewing, as did the introduction of India Pale Ale, which created a significant impetus for home and foreign markets.

Throughout the pages of this book the reader will come across many examples of the contributions made by Scottish inventors, brewers and people in agriculture, which influenced the brewing processes and technical innovations that had a positive impact on Scottish brewing, an industry that developed quite independently, and despite our diminutive population we punched well above our weight.

The process of brewing varied throughout Europe, with the Continentals adopting various methods of decoction mashing whilst the British stuck with infusion mashing. In the UK, brewing is the same south and north of the border but both countries developed the practice in separate ways. For example, the Scots tended to mash and sparge at a higher temperature and ferment at a much cooler temperature, which gave Scotch Ales their unique fullness of character. The English preferred to double mash and ferment at higher temperatures, with the consequence that both styles of beer had different characteristics.

As for hops, both countries used enormous amounts in the eighteenth and nineteenth centuries, which was not so much for flavour but more as a preservative, and it was only during the latter half of the twentieth century that the Scots reduced the hopping rates to a level much lower than that used in English brewing. Also, it was during the late nineteenth century that Scottish mashing and sparging heats and fermentation temperatures, in general, came into line with English practice to increase output in order to compete with English exports to India, Australasia and the wider Empire.

Today, the modern approach to brewing in Scotland is little different from English brewing, and this has been brought about by the new generation of aromatic hoppy beers that are impregnated with floral hops late in the boiling. Consequently, traditional twentieth-century beer styles are a rarity.

HISTORICAL BACKGROUND

'Beer is a very ancient drink – how ancient, nobody can tell, for the time of its origin was before the dawn of history.'
C.L. Duddington, *Plain Man's Guide to Beer*, 1975

Just when and how the natives of the country we now call Scotland started to brew is lost in the mists of antiquity. However, one of the earliest references to brewing in Scotland is in the fourth century BC, when Pytheas of Massalia surveyed the Iberian Peninsula and eventually the coast of Britain as far north as the Orkney and Shetland Islands. He is also said to have visited Thule, which historians consider is either Shetland or Iceland, but the ancients considered Shetland to be the Ultima Thule, being the furthest northern part of the world. Pytheas noted that the inhabitants, the Picts, were accomplished in the art of brewing strong drink and he also gives us an early reference to oaten porridge and the use of oats, heather and honey in brewing.

The 'Picts' is a name given to indigenous Scottish tribes by the Romans and comes from the Latin '*Picti*', meaning painted ones. The Picts were a thriving and energetic people who left their legacy on their exquisitely carved standing stones, which are scattered throughout the land, and their symbols are now thought to be connected to astronomy.

Much of the archaeological evidence is found in Skara Brae at Orkney, which is the best-preserved prehistoric village in northern Europe and is older than Stonehenge and the Egyptian pyramids. Other sites, such as Balfrag in Fife, The Howe on Orkney, at Kinloch Bay on the Isle of Rhum and on the Isle of Arran, tell us that brewing has been carried out in Scotland since Neolithic times. Much of the evidence comes from the residue of both barley and oats that have been detected in shards of broken pottery at The Howe, plus traces of meadowsweet (*Filipendula ulm*aria), heather (Ling, *Calluna vulgaris*), and black henbane (*Hyoscyamus niger*) that were used to flavour the brew. Smidgens of cereal pollen were also found, suggesting the making of mead or ale.[29]

Roasted barley was also found at The Howe and some historians suggest that it was used in brewing, but according to Edmund Burt,[14] and probably prior to cooking, the Highlanders in the 1700s set their barley on fire to get rid of the awn and chaff and so some charring of the grains must have taken place. Presumably the Picts did likewise and so we cannot say for certain that the roasted grains found at The Howe were necessarily used for brewing.

Just how the Picts brewed is open to speculation, and their methods are, like their standing stones, a mystery. However, it was most likely that, like primitive peoples worldwide, they were simply trying to make grain more palatable and digestible and that alcohol was a happy consequence of their experiments. In its raw state grain is hard to chew and digest and so it was soaked in water to soften it, which would initiate germination and the enzymes necessary to convert the starch into sugars. Slow drying by the heat of the cooking fire in clay pots would create crude but palatable malt. To further increase the digestibility and tastiness of the grain, a simple method of mashing, by making gruel in an earthenware 'mash tun', would be essential, and if the pot was sat on the heat of the peat fire sufficient warmth would create a successful mashing and saccharification of the crushed oats or barley, producing sweet porridge. It is most likely that honey, fruits and berries were added to the porridge to add to the nutrient value and to enhance the taste.

However, a common theory is that if all this gruel was not consumed immediately and the remainder of the mash was left overnight by the warmth of the cooking fire, the malt sugars and honey would quickly be fermented by the yeast from the fruit and berries, which was the only source of yeast available to the early Picts, not that they would have a clue as to why this ferment occurred in the first place. Some authors suggest that the gruel was left outside the dwelling to become infected with wild yeast, but the question here is why? Why leave food outside the dwelling where it would be consumed by foraging nocturnal wildlife? Eventually they would separate the stimulating liquid by straining the mash through a perforated animal skin bag held over a shallow clay vessel, and possibly rinsing with hot water.

Some writers have suggested that the gruel left aside for a short period would turn rancid, and this is probably true. However, what might have tasted ghastly to modern man might not have tasted terribly foul to primitive people, and as noted by Dionysius of Halicarnassus in 25 BC, the Gauls used liquor made from barley rotted in water, which was disgusting both in smell and taste.[29]

A boiling vessel would not necessarily be required, as the strained wort would not require boiling prior to spontaneous fermentation by wild and fruit yeast. In this case, flavourings from plants, flowers and wild fruits could simply have been included in the mashing pot, where their flavour and aroma would be diffused into the mash. The use of meadowsweet (*Filipendula ulmaria*) not only flavoured the brew but provided antiseptics to keep it palatable in the short term. Other plants such as belladonna (*Atropa belladonna*), henbane (*Hyoscyamus niger*) and hemlock (*Conium maculatum*) were

also used and induced hallucinations, and their use is thought to be connected with religious practices such as shamanism in placating the spirits.

Should boiling have taken place, it would most likely have been by the ancient method of adding red-hot stones (pot boilers) from the cooking fires, a practice that is still used in Bavaria to produce Steinbier (Stone beer), and this practice would create caramelisation that would contribute to the flavour. A peat fire smoulders and whilst they were fine for cooking, they would not give off sufficient heat to bring a pot to boiling, although it is unlikely that boiling was conducted indoors due to the uncomfortable heat and choking smoke that would fill the low-ceilinged, windowless underground dwellings.

There is also evidence that the Picts waterproofed their vessels internally with bee's wax, and this has been claimed to prevent the seepage of alcohol by evaporation. This is possible but is open to doubt, as it is unlikely that the brew would be stored for long periods as it would quickly go sour. Also, if we take the practice of peoples living in hot countries, they did not glaze their water storage pots so that the slow seepage through the clay evaporated and caused cooling and so the water remained fresh. Skara Brae exempted, the early Picts lived in hill forts, and although there is evidence that they dug shallow wells to collect rainfall, domestic water would have been stored in earthenware pots. Therefore, in the cold northern climate they would be unlikely to require vessels that sweated, causing the loss of such a valuable supply of water, and the waterproofing was necessary to conserve supplies.

During times of drought, water would be acquired from the lower slopes and stored in pots.

The Picts eventually became an organised race indulging in pasturage, and so the art of brewing would have also been well developed. It is claimed that primitive sites of Pictish breweries have survived in Galloway. They are pear-shaped, about 5 metres by 2.5 metres with a side wall of about 1 metre in height, and were built on southern slopes close to running water.[43] Sunken stone troughs were also discovered close to running water and are thought to be cooking (or brewing?) places for game and fish by adding pot boilers. Interestingly, it has also been suggested that the troughs might have been used to steam up primitive saunas.

Knowledge of Pictish brewing can be found on a tenth-century standing stone found at Bullion at Invergowrie in Perth and Kinross, and is now in the safekeeping of Historic Scotland. The stone depicts a warrior drinking from a horn that is adorned with an eagle's head. The eagle's head symbolises power and so the fighter depicted would have been a chief or noble warrior. One wonders, was the warrior drinking an oaten brew flavoured with the corn weed, darnel, or perhaps the fabled Heather Ale?

There are many myths about Heather Ale that have been passed on by oral tradition. One of the most enduring tales is that about AD 375, Niall of the Nine Hostages, the 126th High King of Ireland (died AD 403), crossed the Irish Sea from Antrim to Galloway with a view of exterminating the native Picts and acquire the secret of brewing Heather Ale.

And the fable continues: after a bloody campaign, the only survivors were Trost of the Long Knife, plus his father, brother and the Archdruid Sionach, who had betrayed Trost and threw his lot in with Niall. The victorious Niall had a parley with Trost and offered to spare the lives of his father and brother for the secret of Heather Ale. Fearing that his father and brother might give out the secret under torture, Trost assured Niall that if his father and brother were put to death first, he would reveal the secret recipe. Having sacrificed his father and brother, Trost told the king that he could only reveal the secret recipe to a member of his own race and that he would pass it on the traitor Sionach, out of earshot of the Irish. The king agreed, and Trost led Sionach away along the cliffside. When they were at the steepest part, Trost quickly turned round and grabbed the startled Sionach, shouting, 'The secret dies,' and both men fell over the cliff to their deaths.[62]

It is a marvellous tale, and one wonders what was so important about Heather Ale? The Scots with their Celtic culture, who later inhabited Scotland after ousting the Picts in the ninth century, considered many plants to have magical powers and wore them in their bonnets as talismans to ward off evil spirits and protect them from harm. So, was Heather Ale considered to have magical protective powers and drunk as a libation before battle?

There are many references to brewing Heather Ale in Scotland, principally in the Highlands and Islands, well into the twentieth century. In 1826, James Logan travelled throughout Scotland collecting information of antiquarian interest, which he published in *The Scottish Gael*, 1831. He, too, mentions the brewing of Heather Ale but, interestingly, he also mentions the use of heather roots to flavour the brew, which he claims imparted a liquorice-like taste. It might be that the roots were actually used as a crude strainer in the bottom of the mash tub to filter the wort as it drained from the vessel. Also, Bickerdyke, writing in *Curiosities of Ale and Beer*, 1886, states that heather was used primarily as flavouring and suggests that the taste of the brew was akin to heather honey. Yet, Heather Ale is not exclusive to Scotland – the Irish also brewed Heather Ale, and in Plot's *Natural History*, 1677, we are told that in the district around Shenton, Leicestershire, brewers frequently used *Erica vulgaris* (heather, heath or Ling), to preserve their brews.[44]

Today it is appreciated that heather does not contain any fermentable matter and all references to brewing with it without some form of additional fermentable extract are simply a myth. This fact was evidenced around the turn of the twentieth century, when Dr Maclagan enlisted the help of Andrew Melvin, the son of Alexander Melvin who acquired the Boroughloch Brewery, Buccleugh Street, Edinburgh, in 1850, to carry out a series of brewing trials using heather. Their conclusions were that a brew could not be made with heather alone, but that heather could be used to season a brew just like hops.[29]

The Vikings, too, were also great lovers of ale and controlled Orkney and Shetland, the Western Isles and the north of Scotland from 794 until the twelfth century, and whatever brewing methods they might have had must have survived for some time. They most likely brewed with wild oats or bear/big and flavoured the beer with heather, honey, juniper and rowanberries.

In the early eleventh century, the oldest home brewery in the UK was built at Traquair House, Innerleithen, by Peebles, which was originally a hunting lodge built to provide accommodation for Scottish monarchs and nobility. The beer, which would have been brewed with groot, would have been brewed by the ancient 'cottage system' whereby the cleansing of beer was achieved by simply allowing the casks to fob and overflow and the slops were collected in a vessel below.

It was during the twelfth century that Scotland is reputed to have adopted the German method of brewing, brought here by religious orders, but there is no evidence to tell us just what such methods might have been. It might be, of course, that they introduced the Bavarian practice of long cold storage, or lagering, that became a regular practice in the evolution of Scotch Ale. In 1231, the Blackfriars Monastery was established at Perth and later the site became the Perth Brewery in 1786.

Brewing was largely in the hands of the monks, who had brought the craft to a highly skilled art, and in the thirteenth century the monks of Arbroath Abbey are said to have used more chalders (8 quarters) of malt than all other cereals put together.[43] Such practice would be quite common, as ale formed part of the daily diet and monks consumed up to a gallon of ale a day. Monasteries were also hospices and weary travellers and pilgrims were refreshed with food and ale. It is recorded in the Rental Book of Cupar Abbey, for example, that the monks brewed several ales such as 'Convent Ale', which tells us that the nuns also had their daily tipple! They also produced 'drink of the masses', which would have been their weakest small beer handed out to pilgrims and travellers. 'Household Ale' was brewed for their own use and 'Ostler Ale' for sale to local alehouses and taverns. The strong 'Better Ale' was drunk on special religious days and holidays and was important to sustain the monks during Lent.

The Banff Brewery is said to be the oldest public brewery in Scotland, and production started about 1450–52. During this time the Lowlands was Scotland's main trading partner and much interchange of peoples and goods took place, including beer. Scottish mercenaries also fought for the Dutch, and traders and soldiers would have been well accustomed to hopped beer. It is also claimed that hopped beer was first introduced into Scotland in 1482 and originally brewed by the monks of Banff, followed by the Blackford Brewery in 1488.[8]

The name Blackford comes from the twelfth-century legend when the Norwegian King Magnus lost his wife, Helen, who drowned whilst attempting to cross the ford of the River Allan close by. She was buried at Deaf Knowe near the ford and hence the village became known as Blackford. The Tullibardine Distillery is built on the site of the ancient brewery.

In 1488, when James IV was returning from his coronation at Scone, he refreshed his entourage with the ale of Blackford at 12*s* a barrel, and there is a reference in the Treasurer's Accounts that states, 'quhen the King cam forth of Sanct Johnston for a barrel of ayll at the Blackford'.[8]

In 1493, Bartholomew Bell of Edinburgh was awarded a silver medal by the city's fathers for the quality of his beer.

During the sixteenth century, maltsters and brewers established Maltman Fraternities or Guilds to look after their interests and to control the selling of all goods brought into towns and burghs, and would issue temporary licenses for an individual to sell one specified lot of goods. The coopers of Glasgow, a most important body of artisans, formed The Incorporation of Coopers in 1551, to regulate their trade and look after their interests.

After the decline of monastic brewing, ale and beer was largely brewed for domestic consumption as it was considered safer than well water, which carried a risk of cholera and other water-borne diseases. Surplus ale was sold locally, and in the 1550s the average price of the ale in Dundee was 3/- a gallon (Scots) and lesser quality ale was available as cheap as 1/9*d* a gallon.

The Burgh Magistrates were responsible for the quality, strength and price of the ale and they regularly visited the taverns in their Ward to check that it be 'guid an' sufficient'! The overpricing of ale was frowned upon and carried severe penalties. In Dundee, during July 1562, David Ramsay was caught selling his ale at too high a price, and the Baillies confiscated his mash tun and other brewing utensils and burnt them. He was also forbidden from brewing for one year and a day.

In 1566, Mary Queen of Scots (1525–87) visited Traquair House with her son the future James VI (I) and she no doubt imbibed on Traquair Ale. Queen Mary's reign was an unhappy one, and despite several attempts to reconcile the Catholic–Protestant divide she was captured by the Protestant lords and imprisoned in Edinburgh Castle. Thereafter she was held in

Loch Leven Castle, Fife, and forced to abdicate in favour of her son, James VI. Within a year, Mary made good her escape over the border and threw herself at the mercy of her cousin Queen Elizabeth I, who was well aware of Mary's designs on the English throne and imprisoned her in Tutbury Castle. Whilst imprisoned at Tutbury Castle, Mary acquired a taste for the ale from Burton Abbey, a habit that was to lead to her demise! As she was planning her escape, correspondence was passed out of the castle in the empty casks, which were intercepted by Queen Elizabeth's chief of the secret service, Sir Francis Walsingham, and that signed her death warrant. She was taken to Fotheringhay Castle just outside Peterborough and put to the block in 1587.

In 1573, a new brewery was built at Traquair House that survived until the 1700s. In 1578, John Leslie, the Bishop of Ross, wrote in his *History of Scotland* that English beer brewed with hops was superior to Scots ale brewed with groot, but the latter greatly improved in quality after a few years maturation and acquired the taste and colour of Malmsey. The colour and taste of Malmsey would come from the oxidation picked up through the oak cask during long-term maturation, and so the beer would have had a subtle sherry-like nuance.

In 1596, the Society of Brewers was established in Edinburgh to control and regulate the malting and brewing trades, and in 1605, brewers and maltsters in Glasgow formed the Incorporation of Maltmen (the Malt Craft).

In 1648, we come across an early reference to brewing in Alloa, when Margaret Mitchell is recorded in the Alloa Parish Records as having brewed and sold her home-brewed ale from her house by the Tron Well.[38]

It was the merchants and members of the local trades who ran burgh councils, of which the maltmen were the largest group and they exerted considerable political influence. The councils were self-electing and operated longstanding practices and privileges that gave them total control over the town's affairs. Such political power and control over their fellow citizens inevitably led to much corruption. In 1659, Edinburgh Guildry increased the tax on beer that increased the price of a pint to one penny!

However, the brewers and maltsters were very generous and often came to the assistance of their fellow citizens in time of need. In the Dundee town council minute of 7 December 1669, it is recorded that the maltsters unanimously agreed to pay 2 merks for every boll of malt they brewed to offset the cost of repairs to the town. This was on top of 2 merks Crown duty and their annual membership fees to the Guildry of 40 merks, which was equivalent to £26,13,4*d* Scots, or £2,4,5⅓d English.[21]

In 1690, the Dundee Burgh council again called upon the brewer's generosity, who agreed to pay 10*s* Scots (10/-) for every boll of malt brewed for the next eleven years. The trade-off to this agreement was that the brewers who had previously been barred from holding office in the town council could now do so, and that their annual fee to the Guildry was to remain at 40 merks.

In 1693, Edinburgh Town Council persuaded Parliament to levy an additional 2*d* per pint over and above the King's Excise on every brewer within the town boundaries. The maltsters and brewers argued that the 2*d* tax was intolerable and many existing breweries relocated outside the town's boundaries to escape local taxes. In the same year, the Glasgow magistrates were authorised by Parliament to tax 2*d* per Scots pint to overcome their debts and burdens, and successive Acts of Parliament saw the tax in force until 1837.

In the early 1700s, the present Traquair House Brewery was built, complete with mash tun and fermenting vessels made from the finest Russian Memel oak. Hops would now be used to flavour and preserve the beer.

In 1701, the Dundee council once more applied for aid from the brewers, who agreed to contribute 7,000 merks annually for the next five years.[21] Also, in 1702, Queen Anne sanctioned the town councillors to add an extra *2d* on every pint brewed and consumed within the burgh boundaries. This tax was to be used for repairs to the harbour, the town house and the hospital, and was to last for twenty-four years. The Act specifically stated that the tax was not only to be levied on brewers within the burgh, but also those who brewed in the town's suburbs. In 1706, the price of a pint in Dundee was 20 Scots pennies, which equalled 1 bawbee, or a halfpenny Sterling.

In 1719, Belhaven, Dunbar, Scotland's oldest continually working brewery, was built on the site of an old Benedictine monastery and the wells dug over 700 years ago survived until 1972.

In 1725, we come across another reference to just how small beer tasted in the Scottish Highlands during the eighteenth century, and it comes from *Burt's Letter from the North of Scotland*, by Edmund Burt, a government contractor in the Highlands. Burt does not mention heather, groot or hops, but his description sums up the common ale of the times:

> The twopenny as they call it, is their common ale, the price of it is two pence for a Scots pint. The liquor is disagreeable to those who are not used to it, but time and custom will make almost anything familiar. The malt, which is dried with peat, turf, or furzes (Whins) that gives to the drink a taste of that kind of fuel, it is often drunk before it is cold out of a cap, or 'coif, (Quaich) as they call it.
>
> This is a wooden dish, with two handles, about the size of a tea-saucer, and as shallow, so that a steady hand is necessary to carry it to the mouth, and, in windy weather, at the door of a change I have seen the drink blown into the drinkers face. This drink is of itself apt to give diarrhoea; and therefore,

> when the natives drink plenty of it, they interlace it with brandy or whisky.[14]

The 'change' referred to is the change-house, or tavern. As the brew was drunk whilst still hot and laced with spirits, it was most likely a spiced ale, or toddy, and the fact that it was drunk at the door suggests that it was a *deoch an doruis*, a farewell drink. In non-Gaelic speaking localities the Scots also called a farewell drink a 'stirrup-dram', which has the same connotations as the English 'stirrup-cup'. That the brew should induce diarrhoea might suggest that it was brewed with groot, which could be very laxative.

In Dundee in 1726, which was four years before the expiry of the 1702 Act, the town councillors applied for a renewal of the legislation but did not inform the maltsters and brewers and, consequently, the Act was granted for another twenty-five years! In 1756, further secretive extensions to the above Act were secured, with additional extensions in 1781 and 1802. Such taxes were considered punitive and the Maltmen partitioned Parliament, pointing out that the greater part of the beer brewed in the suburbs was consumed within the burgh free of the tax in question, which contradicted the terms of the Act of Parliament of 1702. The main source of the grievance was against the Pleasance Brewing Company (later to become Ballingall's Pleasance Brewery in 1844) that was sited just outside the burgh boundary, but the bulk of their ales were vended and consumed within the town.[21]

In 1736, an insulated coal-fired copper was installed at Traquair House brewery, which most likely replaced an open cast-iron one, and the wort was chilled in an open shallow wooden cooler before fermentation in one of three fermenters made from Memel oak.

In 1740, Archibald Campbell established the Argyle Brewery in the Cowgate, Edinburgh, a brewery that made a huge contribution to the reputation of Edinburgh as a brewing centre of note, particularly with Scotch Ale and porter.

After Mary Queen of Scots, the next person of note to visit Traquair House was the Young Pretender, Prince Charles Edward Stuart (Bonnie Prince Charlie), who took shelter at Traquair in 1745 during the fateful Jacobite uprising against the Hanoverians. After a brief recuperation, and no doubt emboldened by the fearsome Traquair Ale, he bade his farewells to his host, the 5th Earl of Traquair, and as he departed through the Bear Gates legend has it that as he and his entourage slowly disappeared from view the earl swore that the gates would remain closed until a Stuart was restored to the British throne. This was not to be, and after the 1745–46 Rebellion, which culminated in the disastrous battle of Culloden, the gates remained firmly closed to this day. The Bear Gates, or 'Sleekit Yetts', so called after the carved stone bears that surmount the gateposts, has guarded ten centuries of the comings and goings of kings and queens. Workers who built the house and gates were paid part of their wages with gallons of Traquair Ale.

After the Civil War of 1745–46, Scotland was at peace, and the next fifty years saw major improvements in agriculture and industry. Until this time virtually every tavern keeper brewed their own ale, but due to industry and the wage economy they saw a major shift to large-scale commercial brewing, and by the early 1850s brewing at Traquair House had ceased.

In 1749, Wm. Younger founded the Abbey Brewery in the grounds of Hollyrood Abbey, and it is often claimed that the move was designed to tap into the pure water to be found there, but as the Abbey Brewery was just outside the town's boundary, he was not obliged to pay local taxes. Other breweries that were built within the Palace precincts were Robert Younger's St. Anne's Brewery in 1854, the City of Edinburgh Brewery (1866–74) that was to become Steel and Coulson's Croft-an-Righ Brewery, and J. & G. Pendreigh's Palace Brewery (1865–70).

In Glasgow in 1749, Robert Tennent (future co-owner of Wellpark Brewery) was also a burgess and honourable member of the Malt Craft. Despite this, he was pursued through the Court of Session by the Incorporated Trades of Glasgow for non-payment of local taxes. In his defence he stated that he had kept the White Heart Inn in the Gallowgate for a number of years, where he had carried out his own malting and brewing. Furthermore, he stated that he was tired of paying repeated financial penalties for non-payment of local taxes and appealed to the court to have this stopped. Sitting on the bench, Lord Drummore obviously considered the age-old burghal privileges no longer acceptable and found in Tennent's favour.[20] Six years later, Robert Tennent built the original Saracen's Head (the 'Sarry Heid') using stones from the Bishop of Glasgow's palace that was derelict and falling down.

The Saracen's Head was to become one of Glasgow's most famous and popular taverns, frequented by the wealthy, the literati such as James Boswell and Samuel Johnson, and the aristocratic cock-fighting Duke of Hamilton. It was also the favourite meeting place for the city's magistrates to hold their celebrated dinners, whilst supping Jamaica punch from a five-gallon china punch bowl decorated with the city's coat of arms. Is it any wonder, then, that the magistrates found in Tennent's favour?

By the 1750s, Scottish brewers had established a developing trade with America, Germany, Holland, Poland and wine-drinking Spain, and over fifty-seven barrels were exported annually. Apart from the American colonies, the Baltic ports were fruitful for fledging Scottish brewers. By the middle of the decade exports increased to over 900 barrels.

As the population grew and social conditions improved, areas such as Edinburgh, Alloa and Glasgow developed into major brewing centres. As demand for more beer came from mining and industrial communities, greater demand for good-quality barley resulted in improvements in agriculture, chiefly on the east coast, and East Lothian in particular became known as the grain basket of Scotland. Further north, in Fife, the Mearns, Aberdeenshire and East Ross also became noted for the quality of their barley, although in general Highland barley was grown principally for distillation.

In 1762, George Younger built Alloa's first public brewery, although other sources mention that he was brewing in Alloa since 1744. In 1792, Robert Knox established a Brewery at Cambus, which means 'bend on the river', just west of Alloa. Such was the fame of Knox's beer that he earned the privilege of suppling George III at Windsor Castle. Later the name changed to the Forth Brewery, and by 1845 Alloa could boast eight breweries producing 88,000 barrels per annum.

With the ongoing problem of brewers dodging local taxes, the Edinburgh City Council retaliated against brewers outside the town's boundary by introducing a 2/- Scots tax on all brewers' carts entering the city's boundaries. The brewers responded by delivering their beer on sleighs, but the council quickly included this form of transport in the tax!

The other bone of contention was that burgh magistrates and landowners had the power to issue a degree called 'Thirlage', which was a legal obligation to bind a tenant to grind his malt at a certain mill. The council or landlord also took a toll, or *multure*, of meal for the privilege of grinding the corn at their mill, which was typically one peck on each boll of grain ground. Those that did not comply with the thirlage were to be punished, as the magistrates deemed fit! Until Thirlage and the landlord's right to a multure were abolished, a tenant also had to pay the landlord a duty called *Brew-creesh* for the liberty to brew.

Thirlage, like any other tax, was unpopular and considered punitive, but that did not stop burgh and town officials ruthlessly and mercilessly collected local taxes. In Perth in 1741, Alexander Clunie of the South Inch Brewery (later Muir &

Martin in 1818), James Street, was pursued by the city councillors for multure and excise dues despite the fact that their brewery was sited just outside the town's boundaries.[20] In 1784 at Charles Addison's Brewery, Bo'ness, which was one of the richest in the country with a valuation and stock worth some £7,000, a tax of 2p per pint was slapped on his beer to pay for the upgrading of the harbour.

The beers brewed at this time were either strong ale or weak small beer, but it was only the better off who could afford strong beer and the majority of the population, particularly women and children, drank small beer in lieu of milk. Small beer was a very weak and inferior brew that was produced from the dregs of sugar washed out of the spent grains used for the stronger ales, which was boiled up with the spent hops and fermented. Small beer was eventually called 'twopenny' (*Tuppeny* or *pundy*), which referred to its price around the early eighteenth century, which was 2*d* per Scotch pint; that equalled three English pints, and so it was very cheap. In the Rev. James Somerville's mid-1700s *Statistical Account*, he gives the following description: 'no wholesome beverage could be obtained by the working classes except this thin, vapid, sour small beer'.

The Scots had two distinct types of ale, called common ale and spiced ale, the relative values of which were appraised by law in the following terms. 'If a farmer has no mead, he shall pay two casks of spiced ale, or four casks of common ale, for one cask of mead.' The Scots also brewed Bragwort, a kind of mead made by fermenting ale and honey together. Despite the rise of the public brewer during this time, beer was still brewed by the Scottish nobility, the gentry, tenant farmers and country folk. Monarchs, too, demanded good ale whilst travelling throughout the kingdom.

In 1786, at the outbreak of the French Revolution, the Perth Brewery was established on the former site of the Blackfriars Monastery by local merchants William Wright and maltman

Alexander Ritchie. In 1835, William's nephew, John Wright, became the owner.[64]

As Britain's colonial influence grew, so too did the demand for Scotch Ale from merchants, plantation owners, immigrants and the military, and names such as Younger's and McEwan's of Edinburgh, Calder's and Meiklejohn's of Alloa, and Tennent's of Glasgow became famous throughout the Empire. The introduction of porter in the early 1800s also had a major influence in the overall wellbeing and growth of brewing in Scotland. India Pale Ale also created demand for good ale at home and abroad, and by the turn of the twentieth century the brewing industry in Scotland was second to none.

Of course, brewing, like agriculture, was vulnerable to the fickle Scottish weather, and in the winter of 1822 disaster struck, with a raging North Sea storm that resulted in the Port of Leith being closed due to rough seas, and consequently no coal or barley was landed. Local roads became impassable and coal and grain supplies from the nearby Lothian collieries and farmlands dried up, which shut down the breweries and beer, the staple diet, became very short in supply, bringing misery and hunger to the populace of Edinburgh.[18]

By 1825, there were about 150 public breweries in Scotland producing 588,000 barrels per year, with thirteen in Aberdeen, thirty in Edinburgh, nineteen in Fife, twenty in Angus, fifteen in the Lothians, twenty-two in Glasgow, five in Perth, five in Falkirk, eight in Stirling and six in Alloa. Alongside these were numerous small breweries in county towns and villages.

In 1830, the duty on beer was repealed and taxes on malt and sugar were increased to compensate, and this remained on the statute until 1880.

In 1837, Roberts wrote his masterpiece, the *Scottish Ale Brewer*, which elucidated the latest techniques and thinking on brewing Scotch Ale.

By the 1850s, Scottish brewers were exporting over 21,000 barrels worldwide to Europe, Africa, Asia and America, and by the end of the decade Wm. McEwan in particular had built up a thriving trade in Australasia.

In 1880, the government abolished the tax on malt and sugar, and levied the duty on gravity and volume. It is after this time that we see the introduction of the Shilling terminology, and the 'brewery boom' that followed from 1885 was most productive for Scottish brewers.

At the turn of the nineteenth century there were over seventy-five well established breweries in Scotland. Many brewers were also farmers, maltsters, bakers and innkeepers, and much of this was for reciprocal business expediency often bonded in family nuptials. The farmer, for example, might be related to the brewer, which gave him a secure outlet for his crop and a return of spent grains for his livestock. In some cases, the farmer was also a maltster and so he dealt directly with the brewers, and of course he might also be a brewer and so he had the whole business neatly tied up! The brewer might be related to the baker with a shared supply of yeast, and many brewers were also innkeepers, which ensured an outlet for their beer.

In 1902, Edinburgh City Council sued Edinburgh United Breweries for back payment of the ancient practice of multure, but the case was defended and fell on the fact that no one could say just where the original city boundary actually stood. In early 1900s the brewery boom had turned to bust, as the country slid into depression, although by the recovery prior to the outbreak of war in 1914, Scotland was producing some 2 million barrels per annum.

The twentieth century was to usher in many changes in the Scottish brewing scene, largely due to taxation impinging on recipe formulation, beer gravities and hopping rates. For example, when the Liberal government introduced cost-saving schemes during the First World War, the production of roasted malt and barley was severely restricted to save on energy, and this led to the virtual demise of porter and a severe restriction on stout brewing. The kilning heats for pale malt were also reduced around this time, resulting in paler beers.

Pre-First World War, the duty per standard barrel, which is a cask of 36 gallons at a gravity of 1.055, as opposed to a bulk barrel of 36 gallons of any gravity, was *7/9d*, but by 1917 it increased 21/- and to economise many brewers reduced gravities to save on malt and hops, the latter being very difficult to obtain as the government procured many hop yards for more essential crops. A consequence of this Act eventually led to the Scottish twentieth-century mildly hopped beer tradition. By the end of the war in 1918, the hop crop had shrunk to just under 15,000 acres, with British beer production down to 29,980,000 barrels, whilst the duty had increased to 50/- per standard barrel of 1.055 gravity. Such severe economic cutbacks during the First World War were to have a profound influence on the range of Scottish beer, including strong extra hopped export beers and strong mild that was virtually wiped out.

In 1919, as Britain tried to recover its economy after the war, beer duty was increased to 70/- per standard barrel or 2*d* per pint, and held at this value until 1929–30, when duty rose to a whopping 100/- per standard barrel. To encourage reduced gravities there was a rebate of 20/- per barrel, which led to an average gravity of 1.043. By this time the character of Scottish beers had irrevocably changed, and by the 1920s the range of beer had shrunk considerably; thus 54/- ale of 1.027 gravity; mild ale with a gravity of 1.033; and 60/- ale of 1.037 gravity remained popular with the working class as they were cheap and affordable in small wage packets. Export stout at 1.055, and an 80/- export pale ale of 1.052 remained in vogue, and India Pale Ale and Strong Ale were still produced but with reduced gravities, which were considerably lighter in character than the old Scotch Ale. Scotch Ale did not disappear completely, however, and in the 1920s Wm. Younger's were still promoting their No. 1, No. 2 and No. 3 Scotch Ales for the English market.[34] Also, Dishers 10-guinea ale (210/-), which was very popular in London and the Home Counties, plus Lauder's 10-guinea ale, supporting gravities of 1.100, remained popular. Prices per pint by the 1930s were *5d* for 54/- ale, *6d* for 60/- ale and *8d* for 80/- export.

Overall, beer became weaker and paler, and it was probably during this period that the practice of adding a small top dressing of roasted barley or black malt to the pale ale grist, or caramel in the copper, took place in order to compensate for the loss of the traditional pale-amber colour. However, the percentage of roasted grain added to the grist was never fixed and varied from brewery to brewery. Also, due to the shortage of hops and the lower gravities, the hopping rate throughout the range fell dramatically and, in most cases, only sufficient quantities were used to check the residual sweetness of the brew, which led to Scottish pale ales having a wide range of colour and flavour profiles.

The hop industry fared little better during the post-war years and mildly hopped beers became the norm. However, the bitterness of the hop did influence the overall flavour, and in conjunction with the roasted cereal and residual malt products produced a beer packed with flavour complexity. This style of beer, often categorised within the trade under the Shilling Terminology, remained in vogue until the outbreak of the Second World War, when the average gravity stood at 1.040. The duty at this time was 48/- per standard barrel of 1.027 gravity, plus 2/- per additional degree.

It is also worth pointing out that the whisky industry suffered as well, as Lloyd George introduced the Immature Spirits (Restriction) Act to restrict the consumption of cheap whisky, although spirits for the war effort continued to be distilled. All cereals over and above that required for industrial and military spirits were requisitioned by the government to help feed the population. By 1917, distillation was completely halted. The excise duty per proof gallon in 1914 was 14/9*d*, but by 1918 it had risen to 30/- per proof gallon.

The Second World War saw an inevitable increased in taxes, and in April 1940 the duty per standard barrel of weak beer of 1.027 gravity rose to 65/- plus 2/6*d* per additional degree. In July 1940, the duty was increased to 81/-, plus 3/- per additional degree. In 1942, the duty rose to 118/1½*d*, plus 4/4½*d* per additional degree. As Britain struggled to recover its economy from the war years, the duty in 1946 became 140/7½*d*, plus 7½*d* per additional degree. By 1950, the gravity per standard barrel of 1.027 gravity rose to 1.030 and the duty was 155/4½d.[37, 54] At the outbreak of hostilities in September 1939, the duty on whisky was 72/6*d* per proof gallon, and by 1947 it had risen to over £11.

It was during this period that Scottish brewing underwent further rationalisation to adjust to the post-war economic situation. By this time the shilling terminology had long lost any relevance, and Scottish brewers based their output on three main types of beer: 'light', 'heavy' and 'export'. However, some brewers, such as Ballingall's of Dundee, continued to brew 54/- Ale, no doubt to satisfy the thirst of thousands of mill workers in the city. 'Light' became the successor of mild ale and was invariably dark in colour with an original gravity of 1.030–33. 'Heavy' was a new beer of medium strength, malty and lightly hopped with a sweetish finish and pale amber colour with an OG of 1.037–38. 'Export' became a weaker version of Scotch Ale and India beers, with an OG of 1.040–45.

The 1960s saw further changes within the brewing industry, with the introduction of 'keg' beers that were filtered, pasteurised and artificially carbonated. Such beers were brewed in the Cylindro-conical system, first invented in 1908 by Dr Leopold Nathan and pioneered by the Swiss for lager brewing in the

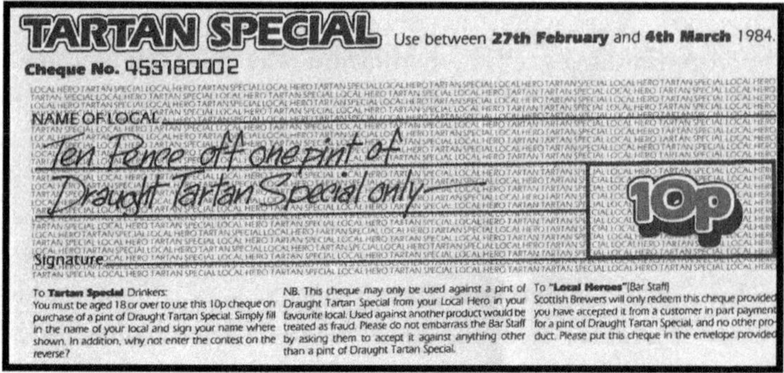

TARTAN SPECIAL Use between **27th February** and **4th March** 1984.

Cheque No. 953180002

NAME OF LOCAL Ten Pence off one pint of Draught Tartan Special only

10p

Signature

To **Tartan Special** Drinkers:
You must be aged 18 or over to use this 10p cheque on purchase of a pint of Draught Tartan Special. Simply fill in the name of your local and sign your name where shown. In addition, why not enter the contest on the reverse?

NB. This cheque may only be used against a pint of Draught Tartan Special from your Local Hero in your favourite local. Used against another product would be treated as fraud. Please do not embarrass the Bar Staff by asking them to accept it against anything other than a pint of Draught Tartan Special.

To **"Local Heroes"** (Bar Staff)
Scottish Brewers will only redeem this cheque provided you have accepted it from a customer in part payment for a pint of Draught Tartan Special, and no other product. Please put this cheque in the envelope provided

1920s. The 'tower' fermenter was an enclosed cylindrical fermentation vessel with a conical base, and early examples were made of aluminium, which it was claimed had no effect on beer flavour. In the 1950s, later models were made of mild steel treated with epoxy resin to protect the beer, and eventually stainless steel.

British brewers did not immediately accept such vessels until the keg revolution in the 1960s, when it was appreciated that they could be used for fermentation and lagering, or conditioning. This saved space in the brewery, as separate conditioning tanks were not necessary. The fact that the CO_2 given off during the fermentation could be easily collected and reused to artificially condition the brew was seen as a bonus. The advantages of bottom-fermenting yeast were that it compacted well and could easily be recovered via a tap on the conical base, and this greatly reduced beer losses. The rate of fermentation was also faster than in traditional fermentation vessels, typically for lagers at 12°C for less than a week and for beer at 20°C for 2–3 days. This meant that brewing capacity was increased, and the vessels were designed with automatic cleaning apparatus *in situ*, which saved time and labour. As the vessels were lagged against heat and cold, they could be sited outside the brewery, thus saving on space.

In 1960, Tennent's took over the rival MacLachlan's Castle Brewery in Glasgow, whose beer was the biggest seller in the city. The takeover also included MacLachlan's Castle Brewery in Edinburgh, and by 1966 brewing ceased in both breweries. In 1961, Wright's of Perth, who previously swallowed up Muir and Martin's South Inch Brewery, James Street, in 1926, were taken over by Vaux and closed down in 1964, and so the Fair City lost a family business and a range of ales and stouts brewed under the supervision of Head Brewer Bob Nimmo. In the same year, Dundee lost Ballingall's Park Brewery, which had been the last independent brewery north of the Tay, to Drybrough's, who closed the brewery down in 1968. In one fell swoop, gone was the popular range of 'Bally's' beers, including Old Bally and Witches Brew, brewed by Head Brewer William McKelvie, who worked his way up the ladder from a brewery labourer in the 1920s and took over from Head Brewer Lt-Col. J.B. Hamilton-Meikle in 1946.

In 1963, Tennent's of Glasgow launched the first draught keg lager and Scottish & Newcastle Brewers introduced Younger's Tartan Special, which is said to be a keg version of McEwan's Heavy. Tartan Special became the beer of Ally McLeod's Tartan Army during the ill-fated 1978 World Cup in Argentina. Two teams that we should have beaten were Iran and Peru, which led to the joke that our other national drink was Iran Peru!

When George Younger of Leckie (who is a direct descendant of George Younger of the Meadow & Candleriggs Breweries, Alloa, 1745) entered Parliament in the 1980s, opposition members kept on pulling his leg by asking for a pint of Tartan Special. In blissful ignorance, they did not realise that he had no hereditary connection with the Wm. Younger of Edinburgh! As the 1960s keg crusade continued apace, Wm. Younger's keg Export and McEwan's Export were introduced.

In 1965, we come across a most important event in the history of Scottish brewing when Peter Maxwell Stuart, the 20th Laird of Traquair, was clearing out the old stables at Traquair House and 'discovered' the ancient brewery below the chapel, which was still largely intact. He sought the advice of Sandy Hunter of the Belhaven Brewery, Dunbar, who enthusiastically provided much guidance, and more importantly Belhaven yeast, and so after 115 years brewing returned to Traquair.

Brewing took place once a fortnight and the brew had an OG of 1.080, producing 8% alcohol, and the laird personally sampled every batch although he insisted that it was only a sip! When bottled, the ale was matured for up to five years, and during a further two years it acquired a degree of acidity and finally resembled port wine. By the 1970s the gravity of the ale was reduced to 1.075 with an ABV of 7.5%.

In 1967, Edinburgh suffered the loss of its last independent brewery, the Argyle Brewery of Campbell Hope and King, Chambers Street. The takeover by the London brewers, Whitbread, caused consternation and anger amongst the beer-drinking public at the loss of this historic enterprise that first brewed in 1710. Campbell Hope and King built up a lucrative tied estate of seventy-three pubs, which were sold to Drybrough's and Vaux/Usher's in 1969, and the Argyle Brewery was closed in 1971. The only remnant of this proud enterprise is that the recipe for Belhaven Best is said to be based on Campbell, Hope and King's 70/- Ale. In 1987, Drybrough's sold out to Allied-Lyons, and brewing ceased immediately at their Craigmillar Brewery, Duddingston. By 1993, only McEwan's Fountain Brewery and the Caledonian Brewing Company remained.

However, by the end of the decade the public had a mood of apathy towards keg beer due to its lack of flavour and excessive gas content, and this led to the formation of the Campaign for Real Ale (CAMRA) in England in 1971. The first Scottish branch was formed in Glasgow in 1974, promptly followed by Edinburgh and Tayside in 1975, and today there are branches throughout Scotland.

CAMRA quickly caught the imagination of the beer-drinking public, and as cask-conditioned ales started to regain their popularity the brewers were quick to capitalise on the renaissance of traditional ales. To emphasise their traditional image, Belhaven Brewers, Dunbar, and McLay's of Alloa simultaneously, but quite independently, revived the shilling jargon and changed 'light' to 60/- ale, 'heavy' to 70/- ale, and 'export' to 80/- ale.

Other brewers were quick to get in on the act, and McEwan's also changed their Export Ale to 80/- ale. Very quickly brewers became enthusiastic, and Wm. Younger re-introduced No. 3 Scotch Ale, which underwent a remarkable metamorphosis from a pale beer with an OG of 1.080 in 1872 down to a gravity of 1.076 in 1896, and finally to a rich dark roast beer in the 1970s with gravity of 1.043! By this time the practice of Scottish brewing had changed to adjust for the lighter gravity beers that the economic situation demanded. The average mash heat became 149°F (65°C) and the hop bitterness in many cases was reduced to a level that simply checked the residual sweetness, although some brewers bucked the trend and hop flavour was more evident, but not so pronounced as the average English ale.

Following on from the keg revolution, we see the introduction of 'continuous fermenters' and various designs were created. In this complex system, hopped wort is aerated in an oxygenating column and is fed in at the base and mixed with some actively fermenting wort. As fermentation proceeds, the partially fermented wort overflows into a second fermenter where the fermentation is finished and again the beer overflows into a yeast separator, where it is cleansed and ready for casking. In the late 1970s, Dryborough's Craigmillar

Brewery, Duddingston, Edinburgh, were the early pioneers with continuous fermentation, but the experiment was short-lived when they were taken over by Allied-Lyons and closed down in 1987.

In 1977, the Laird of Traquair produced Jubilee Ale to celebrate Queen Elizabeth II's (Queen Elizabeth I of Scotland!) Silver Jubilee, and each 9 fld oz bottle was labelled with the Traquair House Ale label but coloured silver and read, 'a potent liquor brewed by the Laird in the Ancient Brewhouse of the oldest inhabited house in Scotland'. This brew must surely signify the acceptance of the House of Windsor, and the Bear Gates can remain securely shut. On 4 October 1978, Traquair's 100th brew was brewed with an OG of 1.075.

As we can see, during the 1960s and 1980s Scotland's brewing industry was decimated, with takeovers and closures. The reason for this steady decline was in part due to the loss of overseas markets after the Second World War, with the British withdrawal from Empire and the growth of breweries in the former colonies. With the writing on the wall, Wm. Younger's closed the Abbey Brewery and converted it into offices in 1955. To add to the misery, some now independent countries imposed prohibitive tariffs on British beer, and this coupled with the austerity that followed left many breweries working below capacity. Consequently, the smaller traditional breweries did not have sufficient capital to invest in the new technologies, which left them in a perilous financial state and the only hope was mergers and takeovers. It is regretted that much of this activity led to the closure of the brewery and the takeover company claiming that there was now too much capacity! Of course, the real reason was simply to acquire the breweries' tied estate and inflate the size of their company.

The following table has been primarily formulated from Donnachie[20] and researches by Gilbert Dallas, and summarises the demise of Scottish breweries from 1955 to 1999:

Location	Brewery	Takeover by	Date	Closed by	Closed
Alloa	Archibald Arrol	Ind Coope	1998	Allied Brs.	1998
	Alloa Brewery				
	Blair & Company	George Younger	1959	Bass	1959
	Townhead Brewery				
	James Calder	Northern Brewers	1960	Bass	1961
	Shore Brewery				
	Maclay & Co. Ltd	Pub Management	1999	Maclay's	1999
	Thistle Brewery				
	George Younger	United Brewers	1960	Bass	1963
	Candleriggs				
	Brewery				
Edinburgh	John Aitcheson	Hammond	1959	Bass	1961
	Canongate	United Brs.			
	Brewery		1960	S&N	1960
	T&J Barnard	Scottish Brewers			
	Edinburgh Brewery		1967	Whitbread's	1970
	Archibald	Whitbread's,			
	Campbell	London	1965	Allied Mann	1987
	Argyle Brewery				
	Dryborough & Co.	Watney Mann	1960	Bass	1992
	Craigmillar				
	Brewery	United Brewers	1958	Watney's	1963
	John Jeffrey				
	Herriot Brewery	Dryborough's	1960	Bass	1966
	George Mackay				
	St Leonard's	Tennent's	1960	S&N	1960
	Brewery				
	MacLachlan Ltd	Scottish Brewers	1960	Bass	1963
	Castle Brewery				
	J&J Morison	United Brewers	1959	Vaux	1960
	Commercial				
	Brewery	Vaux	1960	S&N	1961
	William Murray				
	Craigmillar	Scottish Brewers	1960	S&N	1981
	Brewery				
	Steel Coulson	Vaux	1959	Vaux	1960
	Croft-an-Righ				
	Robert Younger	Scottish Brewers	1960	S&N	1961
	St Anne's Brewery				
	Thomas Usher	Vaux	1960	S&N	1981
	Park Brewery				

Dalkeith	MacLennan & Urquhart Dalkeith Brewery	John Aitcheson	1955	Bass	1958
Dundee	Hugh Ballingall Park Brewery	Dryborough's	1964	Dryborough's	1968
Falkirk	James Aitken Lint Riggs	United Brewers	1960	United Brs.	1966
Musselburgh	John Young & Co. Ltd Ladywell Brewery	Whitbread's, London	1968	Whitbread's	1969
Perth	John Wright & Co. North Methven St.	Vaux	1961	Vaux	1961
Prestonpans	John Fowler & Co. Ladywell Brewery	Northern Brewers	1960	Northern Brs	1962

In the next table we see the range of beers and stouts that were lost with the demise of the above breweries, and the list is probably not exhaustive:

Brewer	Type of beer
Aitcheson, Edinburgh	Best Cellar (bottled)
Alloa Brewery	80/- and 70/- ales
Ballingall, Dundee	Angus Ale, Angus Stout, Witches Brew, Imperial Hopped Ale, 54/- Ale
Belhaven, Dunbar	Export Prize Ale, Bottled Ale. No. 1 Stout, 60/-, 70/-, 80/- and 90/- ales
	Strong Ale bottled 6½ Fld ozs
	Heavy Ale (bottled), Pale Ale (bottled)
Campbell, Hope & King, Edinburgh	Light draught and Heavy, Royal Scotch Ale
Bernard's, Edinburgh	Export, 90/- IPA, Sweet Stout
Deuchar, R., Edinburgh	Export
Deuchar, R., Lochside, Montrose	Ale (draught)
Dryborough, Edinburgh	Burns Strong Ale
	Gold Label Export
	Starbright Pale Ale

Fowler's, Prestonpans	12 Guinea Ale, Wee Heavy (also sold as Belhaven 90/- and Maclay's Strong Ale)
	Brewer's Best Export
	Crown Strong Ale
effrey, Edinburgh	Pale Ale, Strong Ale
	Disher's Strong Ale
	Lager
Mackay's, Edinburgh	90/- Pale Ale (bottled)
	Export
McEwan's, Edinburgh	60/-, 70/-, 80/-
MacLauchlan, Edinburgh	Green Label pale ale (bottled)
MacLennan Edinburgh	Castle Ale, Cameron's Ale, Stout
Steel & Coulson, Edinburgh	Strong Ale
Murray, Edinburgh	Four Guinea Ale
	Wee Murray light ale
	Wee Samson dark heavy ale
Scottish Brewers, Edinburgh	Blue Label Ale, Brown Ale
	Gold Label heavy pale ale, 90/- Sparkling Ale
	Monk Export (bottle) Wee Willie light pale ale
	King of Ales (bottled), Amber Ale
Usher's, Edinburgh	Export, Golden Rule Ale, Red Star Export
	60/- and 80/- Special Export
	Double Maxim Quality Ale
Calder's, Alloa	Strong Scotch Ale, Calder's Lager
James Aitken, Falkirk	Strong Ale
	Highland Pale Ale
Vaux, Edinburgh	Husky Export (bottled)
	Sweet Stout
Younger, G., Alloa	Heavy and Heavy Export Ale
	Treble Top, pale ale
	Stag Brand Ale
	Oat Cream Stout

Younger, R., Edinburgh	Old Edinburgh heavy ale
	XXPS
Wright, J.	Pale Ale, Stout, Sweet Stout, Export
	Barclay Perkins Red Label Stout

In 1982, historians, brewers, maltsters and members of the public became alarmed about the loss of so much history about the brewing industry in Scotland and formed the Scottish Brewing Archive (SBA), which was initially housed in Heriot Watt University, Edinburgh. The enthusiasm for the formation of the archive was very much inspired by the efforts of Mr George Insill, who spent his career as a maltster in Edinburgh and who collected the records of several Edinburgh breweries as they closed down. His collection now forms the core of the Scottish Brewing Archive, which also includes brewing ledgers, photographs, notebooks and objects representing 120 companies and trade associations, including malting and coopering.

By the 1990s Heriot Watt University required more space, and the SBA was asked to move out. The SBA approached the City of Edinburgh council about the setting up of a Brewing Archive and Heritage Centre, but the reaction from the City Fathers was lukewarm. Whether this half-heartedness was for economic reasons or simply indifference, we will never know. However, the responsibility for the future of the SBA now fell on the shoulders of the chairman, Dr David Johnstone, who was the Brewing Director (head brewer) at Tennent's in Glasgow, to find a new home for the archive. He persuaded Glasgow University to accept the care of Scotland's proud brewing heritage, and in 1992 the SBA was transferred from Edinburgh to Glasgow and its future is now secure.

By the end of the twentieth century the proud traditional Scottish brewing industry was all but gone and Edinburgh, which at one time could boast some forty breweries in the nineteenth century, remained at two. To the east at Dunbar, Belhaven Brewery remained buoyant, but sadly they no longer brew cask-conditioned ales. To the west in Glasgow, Tennent's dominated the lager market, and at Alloa, the Burton of the North, which had at one time eight working breweries, tenaciously held on to McLay's Thistle Brewery where the popular shillings ales were crafted under the care of Head Brewer Duncan Kelloch. McLay's Thistle Brewery closed in 1999 in favour of pub management and their beers were brewed for a time by Belhaven Brewery, and latterly by the enterprising Williams brothers in Alloa. In 2005, McEwan's closed the Fountain Brewery and ended almost 150 years of brewing at Fountainbridge. Thereafter, they acquired a stake in the Caledonian Brewery in order to brew their 80/- Ale, principally so that they could still boast 'Brewed in Edinburgh'. Today, McEwan's is owned by English brewer Marston's, and they have stated that they have plans to modify the recipe! The Caledonian Brewery survives but nothing is sacrosanct, and in today's high-powered financial wheeling and dealing we hold our breath…

The saving grace for the Scottish brewing scene came from the microbrewing industry. The seeds of this 'Bier Nuevo' revolution were actually unwittingly sown in the 1960s, when there was a rash of takeovers of Scottish breweries that led to the formation in the UK of the Big Six brewing conglomerates. This led to the virtual demise of the great brewing tradition, and brewery-conditioned beer called 'keg' became king, with the emergence of mega-breweries and tower fermenters that could produce millions of pints per batch or in continuous fermenters. Big was beautiful, and admittedly the technology was admirable except that the beer lacked taste. Rationalisation became the norm and choices were greatly diminished, and by removing individual taste the least number of drinkers were offended. Keg beer was also easy to deliver, as there was no problem with sedimented yeast. The publican had little to do to keep the beer in good condition and to resuscitate this dead brew all he had to do was plug in the cylinders of CO_2. All of this was backed up with huge and expensive advertising campaigns to convince the drinker that in reality, nothing had changed.

Due to the stranglehold of the beer market in Scotland by Scottish and Newcastle Breweries and Tennent Caledonian Breweries, there was limited scope for microbrewers to make significant progress. Consequently, development was slow, but due to the tireless crusade by the branches of the Campaign for Real Ale the public started to respond to the new wave of flavoursome cask-conditioned ales. Many of the early microbrewers were also enthusiastic home brewers who demonstrated that they had the necessary skills to produce excellent beer.

In 1980 we saw the formation of the Small Independent Brewers Association (SIBA), an organisation dedicated to looking after the interests of the microbrewing industry. Some of their successes have been the Guest Beer Provision, which allows microbrewers to gain access to pubs owned by the big brewers. Also, the End Point Duty arrangement, where the duty is paid as the beer leaves the brewery and not, as previously, after Customs and Excise has recorded the gravity and volume.

The introduction of Progressive Beer Duty has meant that small brewers might only pay a tax of 50 per cent. As enthusiasm for microbrewing grew, the industry became more attractive to brewers who had obtained a four-year Brewing Degree at the prestigious Herriot Watt University School of Brewing, in Edinburgh. Also, a number of brewers became disillusioned with their employment in white-jacketed, computer-controlled beer factories, and took up the challenge of craft brewing and running their own business.

As the technologies for microbreweries improved and demand and competition for brewing equipment grew, so prices became more competitive, which allowed many 'lifestyle' businesses to spring up. The practice of maturing beers in ex-whisky casks adds another dimension to the range of bottled beer. Scottish microbreweries produce some very imaginative brews and we see the use of heather, seaweed, gooseberries, elderberries, raspberries, and hopefully in 2021–22 homegrown hops. Scottish hops are a challenge for Scottish farmers in selecting suitable location and soil, plus the erection of a wirework system or poly-tunnels and the building of a hop kiln, otherwise the hops will have to be sent to specialist hop growers in England for drying. It is a tough undertaking and one hopes that some enterprising farmer will rise to the challenge.

The micros initiated a new revolution in brewing. Out went many of the old practices of adding all the bittering hops at the beginning of the boiling and dry hopping in the cask to enhance the aroma. In came early, mid and late hopping, particularly the latter, with lots of the new floral hop varieties that added flavour and aromatics which were liberated into the brew adding spiciness to the palate. The micros also sought out various types of malts from around the globe which further added to the complexity of the brew. Some long-forgotten beer styles from the nineteenth and early twentieth centuries were also revived, and these added to a portfolio of beer that was only a dream thirty years ago.

In the 2002 Budget, the Chancellor gave the microbrewing industry a break by reducing their tax liability by 14p per pint, which was met with glee and encouraged further expansion of the industry. In 2007, we saw the launch of Brewdog in Ellon, Aberdeenshire. Brewdog shook up the UK brewing industry with a range of exotic brews such as Punk IPA, which won the UK's best IPA at the World Beer Awards in 2015. Their classic Cranachan Imperial Stout has a gravity of 1.110, producing an ABV of 11.6!

Today, we see a return to the 'nineteenth century' with some 115 Scottish local breweries in 2017 supplying local, national and international trade. The major brewers have also responded to the craft beer passion and have expanded their portfolio, introducing more appetising beers, some with a hint of Empire, primarily to protect their market share. Such rivalry has beefed up the beer market and increased competition and choice.

In May 2022 Heineken Brewers, owners of the Caledonian Brewery, Est 1869, announced its closure with the beer portfolio to be brewed by Belhaven Brewers, Dunbar.

HOPS AND HERBS

'There is in them a most excellent glance or friendly opening quality, more especially if they were dried in the sun.'
T.A. Tyron, *A New Art of Brewing Beer*, 1691

The name 'hop' comes from an old Anglo-Saxon word '*Hoppian*', meaning to climb. It is a climbing herbaceous perennial with a permanent rootstock called the crown, and has three to five course-textured palmate leaves with sharply toothed edges. The bine has long hollow stems that are square in section and covered with small, hooked prickles that allow it to cling to other plants as it climbs and entwines around them clockwise for support. The hop is allied to hemp or cannabis and nettles in the family of Urticates.

The hop is dioecious and the male flower is very small with short stalks and is borne on many-branched clusters. It has no brewing value but contains the pollen-bearing stamens, which release pollen during July to be carried off with the wind to fertilise any female plants in the vicinity. Such is the polygamous behaviour of the male hop that one plant is sufficient to fertilise up to 200 females!

The female flowers are very small and hidden by the bracteoles that form Brussels-sprout-sized cones. The bracteoles contain the stigma, which is attached to the ovaries, and once fertilised by the windborne pollen grains forms the seeds of the next generation. As the hop ripens, the bracteoles become

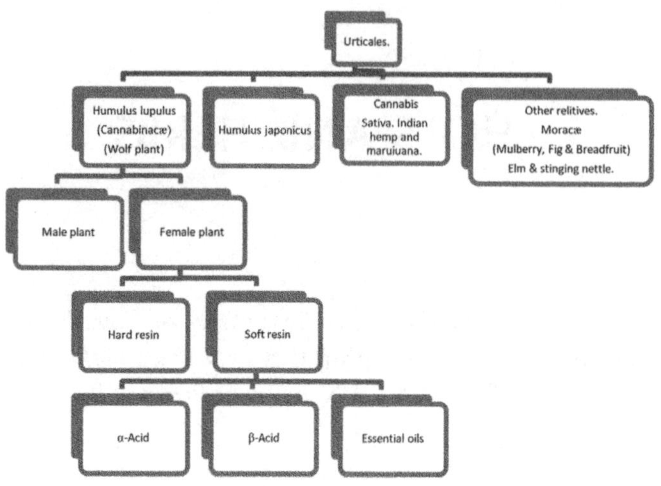

loose and somewhat papery and rustle noisily in the wind. The hop is a natural diuretic and soporific and the use of a hop pillow is well known.

The rootstock can grow up to a depth of 30ft (10m) and grows best in a deep well-manured soil with good drainage. The type and quality of the soil will influence the quality of the hop and some soils are more suited to one variety than another. The soil in the Faversham district of Kent, for example, has a light loam over a brick earth, which historically was best suited to Goldings and Bramblings. Mid-Kent has a similar loam over ragstone, that is best suited for the Fuggle, although Bramblings and Goldings are also grown and in the Weald of Kent the loam is over clay subsoil, ideally suited to the Fuggle. The soils of Worcester and Herefordshire are much heavier and the Brambling and Fuggle survive best here, although the yields per acre can be some 2 cwt-per-acre less than in Kent.

The hop-growing counties of Surrey and Hampshire centred on the district of Farnham, which is known for its deep loams, which are very suitable for hop growing. They produced the superior and famed Farnham Pale, a hop much sought after by Scottish brewers during the nineteenth century due to its fine qualities. Hops were also grown in Nottinghamshire, which has heavy clay soil, and the hops were referred to as North-Clay hops, which had a strong undesirable rank flavour described as 'bordering on the nauseous'! Consequently, they were only suitable for strong stock ales boiled in an open copper that allowed the rankness to vent.

The weather also has an influence on the on the size and welfare of the crop. Whilst hops require a good deal of rain during the period of active growth during May and June, a dry summer is best suited for Goldings, and growers referred to such conditions as a 'Golding season'. Should the summer be a wetter one, which is more favourable for the Fuggle, the farmer called it a 'Fuggle season'.[48]

By the early eighteenth century, the hop was recognised as being more wholesome to beer and healthier than other bittering materials. Consequently, in 1710 the government brought in the Hop Tax at 1*d* per pound for homegrown hops and 3*d* per pound on all imported hops, and the common brewer, innkeeper or victualler was banned from brewing with broom, wormwood or any form of groot. By banning the use of groot, which was not taxed, the government would hope to secure more revenue from the use of hops. One of the earliest mentions of hops in Scotland is in Dundee in 1734, when the Guildry issued a licence to a stranger visiting the town for 18/-, which allowed him to sell the hops he had brought with him.[21]

On top of the cost of the hops and taxes, Scottish brewers also had to reflect on the cost of importing hops. For example, in 1809 the freight cost by sea for hop bags (2½ cwt) and pockets (1¼ cwt) from London to Dundee was 4/8*d*, whilst the cost of importing a hogshead of porter, ale and beer was 7/-. By 1818 the freight cost of ale, beer and porter remained at 7/-, whilst hops in bags rose to 14/- and pockets rose to 16/-. By the twentieth century, hop bags, which were used for courser hops intended for stouts and porters, were discontinued and the hop pocket was standardised at 1½ hundredweight. German hops were exported in round bales and American hops in rectangular bales.

The most obvious way to overcome this huge financial outlay was for the Scots to grow their own hops, and although many had doubts about such a venture, early trials looked promising. Writing in the *Gentleman Farmer* in 1776, the Scotsman H. Hume stated, 'If I can reduce the expense within moderate bounds, I am not afraid of the climate in Scotland; many judicious trials made here have produced good hops.' However, hop growing in Scotland did not become well established until the 1860s, with hop gardens in five counties reaching as far north as Aberdeen by 1870.[16,48]

Ultimately, however, the Scottish climate was not ideal for hop agriculture, with late frosts and accompanying hailstorms that were quite common during June and July in the nineteenth century, and could wreak havoc on the young crop. Also, the damp 'driech' climate was favourable for the development of Downy Mildew and Hop Mould, plus a host of other funguses and viruses, which can quickly destroy the crop. On top of all of these were the high cost of the elaborate pole and wirework supports and the labour required to maintain them. Consequently, hop growing was abandoned in 1871, but remnants of this industry can still be found growing wild in woodlands and quiet byways.

The amounts of hops added per quarter of malt or barrel of beer varied enormously in the old days. The quantity of hops also changed throughout the year, as the brewer blended in new hops with the old to balance out the bitterness and achieve a degree of consistency. Spent hops were regularly reused in weak beers or pundy. In 1873, Younger's brewed a stout that consisted of 35 per cent five-year-old American hops. This is interesting, as brewers up to this time considered that hops deteriorated by 25–30 per cent during the first year of storage, and so by five years they must have been pretty useless. Such 'yearling' hops will have lost so much of their aromatic principles to make them unusable for the better quality pale ales, and we can see why they were employed in stout. However, it is also recorded that in the 1930s, good-quality Worcester hops were kept in cold storage for eight years and were found to be in good condition.

The spicy complex flavour of the hop is transient and only lingers until the beer is swallowed. Hops also contain narcotic principles, more so in course hops, and Dr Emil Westergaard spoke of 'morphine-like alkaloids in the hop leaf'. Strong India Pale Ales demanded a high hopping rate to provide ample antiseptics from the α-acids to preserve the brew on its long sea voyage to India, which included crossing the heat of the equator twice.

In Robert's day the hops were added in two stages to 'obtain for the finer ales the more delicate flavour of the hop'. In the 1850s, J. & R. Tennent's ales were noted for their remarkable keeping quality and the retention of that delicate flavour of the hop. Also, when the Victorian brewery historian, Alfred Barnard, visited Ballingall's brewery in Dundee, he described their special pale ale as being, 'as delicious as any we have tasted, without being heady it is highly nutritious, bright and sparkling, and tastes well of the hop'. There should be no doubt, therefore, that Scottish beer in the eighteenth and nineteenth centuries had a hoppy character. Charles Henry Cook (1858–1933), writing under the pen name John Bickerdyke, wrote that Scottish brewers were great believers in malt and hops.

The early varieties such as Meophams and Prolifics proved adequate, and although the latter was a heavy cropper it was lacking in soft resin and therefore of poor brewing value, and was primarily used to perk up old hops. By the early eighteenth century, the finest pale hop was the delicate Farnham Pale, also known as Surrey Bines, which was eventually grown in Kent. By 1795 we see the introduction of delicate hops such as East Kent's (Goldings) and Worcester's, with tantalising flavours and aromas. Less prized hops such as Colgate's (1805), Jones's and Fuggles (1875) were reserved as copper hops. In general, the Scots preferred aromatic hops with delicate flavours, and varieties such as North-Clay hops were rejected as they had a strong objectionable flavour. By the 1850s Scottish brewers made much use of Kent's, East Kent's, Farnham's and Oval's.

In 1862, the hop tax was abolished and brewers' licences were increased to compensate for the loss of revenue. Many Scottish brewers also became hop merchants, and 1872 Ballingall & Son, Brewers Dundee, were also hop importers and would have supplied much of the local trade. At the same time, the aptly named William Hopkins was the agent for Strauss & Co., Dundee, Hop Merchants, located at India Buildings. Of course, some brewers dealt directly with the English hop merchants, and Wm. Ure of the Hawkhill Brewery, Dundee, dealt with Pike and Sons, Hop Merchants, London, and also Fluer & Maye, Hop and Malt Exchange, Southwark, London.[2]

In 1894, hop breeding started at Wye College at Ashford, Kent, but by the end of the nineteenth century Scottish brewers were importing hops from Bavaria, Belgium, France, Czechoslovakia and America. Many imported hops, however, were of a poor quality, with the pockets containing much dead leaf, strig and extraneous matter. By the twentieth century, Kent Goldings and Fuggles became the dominant varieties employed by Scottish brewers. In 1914, the area under hop cultivation in England was about 35,676 acres, producing about 559,000 hundredweight of hops to brew roughly 37,684,000 barrels of beer throughout the UK.

Some old and largely forgotten favourites were Petham Golding, Copper hop, Early Choice, Pride of Kent (which was crossed with a Tasmanian male hop to produce Pride of Ringwood), Concord, College Cluster, Mayfield Grape, Malling, County Farnham, William's Hops (1780), Jones Hops, Midseason, Prolific Hops and Sunshine. The latter was a Wye hop crossed with an American male hop to produce Comet hops. Oval hops were also popular in Scotland and were much used by Wm. Younger. There is also the oriental ornamental hop *Humulus japonicus*, which does not produce resin and has no brewing value. At Wye College, Prof. Salmond raised several new varieties by crossbreeding with American high α-acid hops, and between 1938 and 1944 saw the introduction of Bullion, Brewer's Gold and Northern Brewer. Northern Brewer was readily accepted due to its high α-acid content with good flavour and aroma. It was named as a tribute to Wm. Younger's of Edinburgh, who conducted trials during the Second World War.

Bullion and Brewer's Gold were not so popular due to the strong 'American flavour' that resembled blackcurrants. However, Bullion, Brewer's Gold and Northern Brewer became very popular in German hop-growing districts, as they were found to be more resistant to German strains of Verticillium wilt. Of course, for the past seventy years or so this trend has continued, with a variety of high resin aromatic hops well known to brewers worldwide. In 1995, Prof. R.A. Neve bred the first dwarf hop, First Gold, which was a cross between Whitbread's Golden Variety (WGV) and a dwarf male hop, and so the quest for the perfect hop goes on. During Neve's time at Wye College, consideration was also given to naming a hop, 'Wye Not!'

Of course, in the nineteenth century global warming was unheard of, but today we experience climate change and so the warmer conditions in Scotland are much more suitable for hop growing. Also, with modern agricultural techniques and more robust strains of dwarf hops grown under polytunnels, the future looks bright for hop growing in Scotland. Successful trials have already taken place at the James Hutton Institute, Invergowrie, Perthshire, on the outskirts of Dundee, with First Gold and Pioneer. In 2015 a small batch of craft beer, called Local Hero, was successful brewed for the Institute by the St Andrews Brewing Company in Fife. Current varieties grown under field conditions are First Gold, Pioneer, Styrian Goldings, Perle and Phoenix, and Scottish craft brewers await the results with enthusiasm.

Before the introduction of hops, the following plants were either used singularly, or mixed in various proportions with other plants, including hops, to make groot that must have changed regularly with the seasons, which meant there was no consistency in the flavour of the beer.

Yarrow (*Achillea millefolium*) Yarrow is a common wild flower found in hedges and roadsides throughout Britain. In an old Gaelic chant a woman sings: 'I will pick the green yarrow that my figure may be fuller, that my voice will be sweeter, that my lips will be like the juice of the strawberry, I shall wound every man, but no man shall harm me.'[51]

Pennyroyal (*Mentha pulegium*) A close relative of mint, Pennyroyal has also been used as a great cure-all and insecticide.

Thyme (*Thymus praecox*) The wild mountain thyme, a favourite culinary herb that also formed part of groot.

Darnel (*L. Temulentum*). A poisonous weed that grows amongst cereal crops. It was reputedly used by the Picts to flavour beer, which probably accounts for their demise!

Heather (*Calluna vulgaris*) (Gaelic, *Fraoch*) Heather, or Ling, is a short stubby plant that covers large tracts of land in Scotland, and is most common in boggy areas and on moors with poor, or acid, soil. The flowering period is from August to September and it is quickly spotted by its purple flowers. This is the most common type of several species of heather and the Highlanders made many uses of it such as brewing, thatching, rope and broom making. It was also used to make a dye for tartan and produced yellow, green and brown.

Bog Myrtle (*Myrica gale*) (Gaelic, *Roid*) Bog Myrtle is a shrubby plant with reddish stalks and tooth-edged coloured leaves of grey-viridian. It grows in bogs and wet heaths forming large aromatic clumps. It is actually very difficult to spot unless one knows exactly how to recognise it. The flowering period is from April to May. It is also known as Sweet Gale, and it was used throughout Europe to flavour beer. It has been suggested that 'gale' might derive from the word 'gall', which refers to its bitter qualities. Or, perhaps, from the Norse 'gayr', meaning 'foolish', referring to the highly intoxicating qualities of the beer that it flavoured.[50] Highlanders used the plant to produce a range of colours such as yellow, yellow-brown, yellow-green and orange. They also put Bog Myrtle in their bedding to keep fleas at bay, and Boy Scouts crushed the leaves inside their tents so that the eucalyptus-like aroma acted as an insect repellent.

Gorse (*Ulex europaeus*) (Gaelic, *Conas*) Gorse is also known as Furze, but more commonly referred to as Whin.

It is a dense shrub that grows to about 2 metres in height and flowers during spring and summer, although in favourable conditions it might flower for most of the year. Country winemakers have long used the bright yellow flowers to make an interesting wine. The flowers are protected by sharp barbs that makes them difficult (and painful!) to harvest. Consequently, just how much was actually used in brewing is open to question.

Broom (*Cytisus scoparius*) (Gaelic, *Bealaidh*) Broom is similar to gorse but without the spikes and grows in similar acid, sandy heath. It too was used to produce yellow and green dyes and it is the cap badge of the clan Forbes and MacKay. The bright yellow flowers are borne on young shoots during April and June. Both broom and gorse are known to induce the symptoms of intoxication in sheep, and so combined with alcohol the brew would be quite stupefying! The seeds also contain small amounts of the poisonous alkaloids sparteine and cytisine and the glycoside scoparin. Also, in *First Steps in Winemaking*, the author casts doubt on the safety of broom for winemaking, although Broom Ale is mentioned in old brewing texts.

Wild liquorice (*Astragalus glycyphyllos*) (Gaelic, *Carmeal*) Commonly called Milk Vetch, as it is said to increase the milk yield from goats that grazed pastures where it grew. In brewing, the roots were bruised and infused with hot wort and fermented to produce Cairm Ale. Milk Vetch should not be confused with its close relative *Glycirrhiza glabra* that is used in confectionery, or *Ononis repins* (Restharrow) that is also called wild liquorice. All species can be used in brewing and chewed to extract the warm pungent flavour.

Meadowsweet (*Filipendula ulmara*) (Gaelic, *Lus-Chuchulainn*) The name 'Meadowsweet' is a corruption of the original name 'Medesweet' as it was used to sweeten honey wine or mead. It is a perennial plant that grows to about 2 metres high, and the flowers are borne on long frothy sprays and bloom from June until September. Meadowsweet is often called 'Queen of the Meadow' as it has a sweet aroma and grows best in marshy ground and meadows, and is often found close to running water. This fact is interesting, for we know that Pictish breweries were also built close to running water and Meadowsweet was used in brewing at Skara Brae. Meadowsweet contributed to the flavour, but also contains salicylic acid, which is in large quantities poisonous, but in small amount acts as a preservative and antiseptic.

Mugwort (*Artemisia vulgaris*) A fairly common plant found by the roadside and hedgerows. It grows to about 1.2 metres tall, often forming large tufts. It flowers from July to September and has a light 'honeycomb' aroma. It has a mild bitter taste and was infused in the wort until the required degree of bitterness was achieved.

Norway spruce (*Picea abies*) The Norway spruce is none other than the familiar Christmas tree that became popular in Britain after Prince Albert brought one back from Germany for Queen Victoria. Spruce beer is popular in Scandinavia, and as the Vikings ruled the Western Isles and Caithness and Sutherland until the twelfth century, the idea of using spruce tips in beer may have come from them. During the French and Indian Wars, Scottish troops became accustomed to supping Spruce Beer. In 1845, Spruce Beer was imported into Perth from Danzig and was subjected to a duty of £1 per barrel and harbour dues were 2*d* per keg. Spruce Beer was also recognised by seafarers as treatment for scurvy and is mentioned in James Lind's *A Treatise of the Scurvy*, 1753.

Dandelions (*Taraxacum officinale*) (Gaelic, *Bearnan Bride*) 'Dandelion' comes from the French 'dent de lion', meaning lion's tooth, and refers to the angular shape of the leaves that look like lion's teeth.[53] The dandelion is also known as 'Doon-head' or 'Clock' or Milk-gowan. Dandelion florets are used in country winemaking and the leaves, which are rich in vitamin C, are used in salads. The dandelion has also been used as a diuretic in herbal medicine, hence its nickname, 'pee the bed'! The dried and ground roots make an ersatz coffee and they were also infused with orange peel in beer to make 'Het ale' (hot spiced ale), traditionally served in a tappet hen.

Nettles (*Urtica dioica*) (Gaelic, *Deanntag*) The common stinging nettle has been used in brewing and homeopathy since ancient times and was used in the treatment of rheumatism.

Ginger (Fam. *Zingiberaceae*) Ginger is a tropical perennial plant native to South East Asia, and due to the popularity of the sub species, *Zingibir officinale*, as a culinary spice it is now grown worldwide. Ginger has fat knotty tuberous roots with a pungent spicy flavour, which was also used in groot brewing and in alternative medicine for stomach upsets.

Elderberry (*Sambucus nigra*) The elder tree contains sambunigrin, which is a glycoside found in the leaves that breaks down during hydrolysis to glucose, benzaldehyde and prussic acid, which is known to cause nausea and vomiting if not destroyed at a temperature above 80°C. It is important, therefore, that only the flowers and berries are used and that the leaves and stalks are rejected. The flowers and berries are a rich source of vitamin C.

Rowan (Mountain ash, *Sorbus aucuparia*) (Gaelic, *Caorunn*) 'Rowan' is derived from the Norse '*runa*', meaning a charm. Rowan branches were often hung above the main door to ward off witches, and above the byre to prevent the milk from becoming bewitched, and milkmaids would drive the cattle to and from the shealings for summer grazing with a rowan rod to protect them from evil. Rowanberries contain small amounts poisonous prussic acid, although they have been made into enjoyable edible products such as a sharp jelly to accompany game. They also make a pleasant country wine, an interesting liqueur and Rowan Ale, and the later was said to be the favourite tipple of Samuel Pepys. The plant flowers during May and the bitter berries ripen during September and October.

Quassia bark (Fam. *Simarubaceae*) The name Quassia comes from the name of the native called Quassi, who discovered its value as a tonic against fever. A wash of Quassia and soap was also an effective fungicide for destroying aphids on the hop bine in the nineteenth century. Dried chips of the bark of the South American tree Quassia Amara have been used as a hop substitute during the eighteenth, nineteenth and early twentieth centuries. The typical quoted quantities are that 1 pound of bark produced the equivalent bitterness of 16 pounds of hops. As Quassia and other non-hop bitters are poor antiseptics, the quantities used rarely exceeded one third of the hop grist.

The hop substitutes used in the nineteenth century were Calyso, a bitter non-narcotic herb that was more wholesome in beer than one brewed with hops and was also considered to have about the same antiseptic qualities. One pound of Calyso equalled 12 pounds of hops. Chiretta is a member of the *Gentianaceae* family and native to Northern India. One pound of Chiretta was equal to 10 pounds of hops. Gentian is a bitter plant, of which 1 pound equalled 7 pounds of hops. Whilst the foregoing had adequate bitterness, apart from Calyso they did not have the same antiseptic values as hops and brewers were advised not to substitute no more than one third of such bitter in place of hops.[56]

Coriander seeds (*Coriandrum sativum*) Coriander seeds were also used in Scotland in conjunction with groot and hops and add a degree of pungency to the brew. Historically, 1 pound per bushel was the ratio, but amounts between 2–4 grams per litre should be good for starters, and they may be added whole or crushed during the last fifteen minutes of coppering or added to the FV. In nineteenth-century Scotland, coriander seeds were also coated with sugar and given to children as sweets.

Honey was used well into the nineteenth century as a source of extract and it would influence the flavour of the brew. It consists of glucose and fructose and is 100 per cent fermentable, and so it would not add sweetness to the brew.

NINETEENTH-CENTURY BARLEY AND MALTING

'That fruits and herbage may our farms adorn, and furrowed ridges teem with loaded corn.'

Robert Ferguson (1750–74)

It is a fact that there are some 100,000 different varieties of barley grown throughout the world, and they are placed in the genus *Hordeum*. Not all strains are suitable for brewing and the two most important for the brewer are *H. vulgare* and *H. distichon*. It is thought that barley came to Britain after the Phoenicians found a way out of the Mediterranean via the Straits of Gibraltar during the eighth century BC, and they eventually sailed to Baratanic (Britain) and traded barley for Cornish tin. In Scotland during the Middle Ages common oats (*Avena sativa*), which were believed to have originated in Asia, were in common use.

Common wheat and barley were grown and used in brewing, but from the 1600s onwards coarse six-rowed Celtic barley such as 'bear' (*Bere* or *beere*) became popular. Coarse four-rowed 'Big' (*Bigg*), which is believed to have come from Iceland, was also cultivated and was also known in some areas as 'Chester-barley'. Both strains can survive in poor soil and at high altitudes, which made them ideal for the Scottish climate.

Both types, however, had small pickles (the ear) and a course thick husk, which is fine for mash tun roughage but would not have produced a high extract. Despite the introduction of superior two-rowed barley, four-rowed barley remained the principal crop well into the seventeenth century.

During the seventeenth and eighteenth centuries, the common method of cultivation in Scotland was the run-rig system, which consisted of broad strips of raised arable land about 5–10 yards (5½ –9 m) in width and running the length of the field. The raised beds allowed the soil to drain naturally into the lower furrows that kept the crops from becoming waterlogged. The time of sowing, which depended on the locality, was from early April until mid May, using some 8–14 pecks (64–112lbs) per acre.

Due to population increase and more mouths to feed, the run-rig system slowly died out and the rigs were ploughed flat to increase the acreage and crop yield. Before the introduction of horse-drawn sowing machines in 1867, sowing was done by 'broadcasting', a primitive method whereby the grain is thrown to the left and right by alternate hands from a basket slung from the neck. A later development was the 'Seed Fiddle', an ingenious device that was also slung from the neck and operated by a

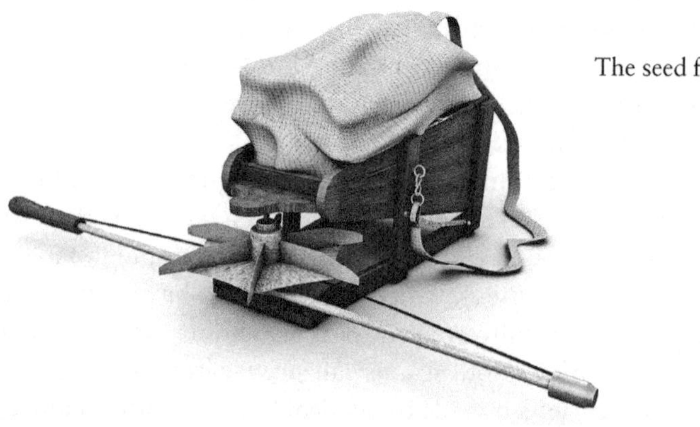

The seed fiddle.

string and bow. The string was secured at both ends of the bow and turned once round a central spindle. Attached to the spindle were a series small of hollow projections through which the grain would flow from the seed container, and as the bow was worked to and fro it turned the spindle and the grain was forced out by centrifugal force and spread in a semi-circle.

When the grain was ripe in the autumn it was cut either by a sickle or by a scythe, an implement that was introduced by the Romans. Harvesting with the sickle was backbreaking work and only a quarter acre could be harvested in a day. The use of the scythe was just as labour intensive, although a larger swathe could be cut with each swipe and as much as an acre could be reaped in a day. The loose crop was now gathered into neat bundles called 'stooks' (sheaves) that were secured with strong twine and tied off in a 'corn-knot'. A 'binder' or 'stooker' was the name given to the worker who gathered the stooks, and he would arrange 6–8 sheaves 'stook-ways' by leaning against each other to form an 'A', which would allow air to flow through the stooks and dry the grain.

In 1826, Scotsman Patrick Bell invented a horse-drawn binder that automatically cut the corn and bound-up the stooks. This was a great labour-saving device, as only one man was required to control the horse and binder whilst the sheaves were stooked by a couple of stookers.

After the harvest the stooks were allowed to remain in the field for about two weeks to mature and dry out. Next, they were taken to the stack yard. Stacking the corn was a work of art and each sheaf would be laid stook-ways in a circular fashion with the heads of grain innermost. The stack was built around a tripod that would allow a continuous airflow in the stack, which would keep the stack dry and prevent it from overheating by microbial activity. On average a stack would be about 15ft high by 20ft wide (4½m by 7m). The stack was finished off in a cone with the stooks laid in a thatch-like fashion to keep the stack dry. To secure the thatching, the stack was covered with large netting of rope with tails hanging down attached to heavy stones.

The harvest time was a period of long hours and backbreaking work, and after the harvest was in there was a mood of jubilation and the community celebrated the 'stooking' with a festival, which might be known as a 'bear-barrel', a 'kirn' or a 'meal and ale' in the barn or village hall. The festival usually opened to the sound of the bagpipes and the people danced to accordion and fiddle music. The farmer might also brew Harvest Ale and those who could afford it brought along a half-cutter of whisky, and the festivities usually lasted until the crack o' dawn. A fair bit o'courting also took place and many life-long relationships were formed. The dance was ended to the sound of the bagpipes ... providing that the piper was not too 'fou'!

When the grain was required for use it first had to be threshed to separate the pickles from the sheaf and separate the husk (the shell, shiel or chaff) from the 'groats' (the inner kernel). In primitive times this was achieved by simply rubbing the kernels between the hands, or flailing the sheaves with supple branches of birch or rowan. A later idea was the 'hogs back', which was a board set out with a number of spikes through which the sheaf was drawn to detach the kernels.

The next stage was to separate the chaff from the groats, which was achieved by throwing the grains in the air, allowing the heavier groats to fall to the ground, but the lighter shiel particles would be blown away in the wind. To achieve the same end, the ancient brewery at Skara Brae was constructed so that the chamber had an opening at each end that could be opened as required to catch the prevailing wind and blow the chaff away.[29] When stone barns were eventually built, they often had doors on each gable, which would be opened when required to provide a through draught when winnowing.

The process was made easier with the introduction of the 'wecht', which was an animal skin or canvas, stretched over a wooden hoop made from birch or rowan. The wecht kept the grain off the ground and reduced losses and it was operated by two wechtmen. This practice is known as 'winnowing', and it was traditionally carried out at a known windy spot usually on high ground and consequently we come across localities, or farms, known as 'Windyhill', 'Shillinghill' and 'Shielhill'.

The laborious winnowing lasted until 1758, when Michael Stirling of Dunblane invented a threshing device based on a water-driven flax mill. In 1786, Andrew Meikle (1719–1811), a millwright from Dunbar, East Lothian, invented the threshing machine in which horses walking round a circular gearing drove the mills that consisted of several flails thrashing the grain from a revolving axle. Later, the threshing mill became more efficient, driven by wind, steam or water, although in many cases horse-power remained in vogue well into the nineteenth century. As not every farmer could afford a mill, those that had one hired it out and it was transported from farm to farm pulled by a team of Clydesdales. Later, the horses were replaced by the steam traction engine that also powered the mill.

Historically, brewers simple made do with native barleys that had no known pedigree, and indigenous barleys in the UK were Scotch Common, Annet, Old Wiltshire, Old Cornish, Old Irish, Early Welsh and Nottingham Long Ear.

During the 1700s, Annat and Scotch Common become the principal crops used in Scotland, and Scotch Common was particularly suited to the Scottish climate due to its early ripening characteristics and it became the mainstay of the Scottish malting industry. Wm. Black of the Devanha Brewery, Aberdeen, preferred Angus barley that was possibly two-row, although it was sometimes blended with expensive Norfolk barley to achieve superior wort.

Due to a succession of bad harvests that threatened farmers with ruin, the Corn Laws were introduced in 1815 to safeguard the interests of farmers and the gentry. This led to the importation of grain being prohibited as long as the average price was below 80/- per quarter. In practice the Corn Laws encouraged the exportation of grain that reaped huge profits for the landowners at the expense of the poor. Much of the grain went to the French, and as there were still bitter memories of the Napoleonic Wars much rioting broke out and the Anti-corn League was formed in Manchester in 1839. The Corn Laws were abolished in 1846.

A major improvement in the quality of brewing malt in Scotland came in the early nineteenth century with the introduction of two-rowed Chevallier barley from England, which has an interesting history. The story goes that in the autumn of 1820, farm servant John Andrews was resting at home after a day at the threshing and found some grains in his sweaty socks! He is said to have considered the grains to be particularly fine and out of interest he planted them in his garden at Debenham in Suffolk. Thereafter, his landlord the Rev. Dr John Chevallier was paying a visit to inspect his property when he spotted the ripe barley growing in John Andrew's garden. He too thought that barley looked fine and decided to cultivate them on his farm to see what might result. The first batch produced a superb crop, so he increased the area regularly until he had an acre, and by 1825 he had a sufficient number of bushels for sale. Eventually this strain became famous as Chevallier barley and was a great favourite for malting.

In reality, the Chevallier barley must have been one of the many types of native barleys that evolved through natural cross-pollination and was a regular crop on the farm where John Andrews worked. It is a fact that the best barleys are grown on light, warm, friable soils, and it is interesting that Chevallier prevailed so well in the heavier soils of Suffolk.

A more plausible story would have been if the barley was spotted growing wild in some quiet byway by Dr Chevallier, or that he simply took a rip from the crop, but like all tales the legend is always better than the fact.

In time, a variety of selections of Chevallier were cultivated at home and abroad, and the Scottish cultivar became known as Scotch Chevallier, which became the principle malting barley grown in the best agricultural districts of Scotland. Scotch Chevallier had nice plump ears, a thin husk that limited the amount of astringent tannins and silica. Chevallier typically produced an extract of 106lb per quarter and was to dominate the malting scene until 1889, when an improved strain, the 'Goldthorpe', was developed from Chevallier at Goldthorpe in Yorkshire.

In 1905, E.S. Beaven cross-pollinated the wide-eared Danish variety 'Plumage' and the narrow-eared type 'Archer' to produce the first genetically true British barley, Plumage Archer. It was a barley that was suitable for growing on heavy richer soils and was characterised by low nitrogen (protein) and a high yield of about 108 brewer's pounds per quarter, and became the dominant malting variety for the next fifty years. It is still grown today, organically, on Prince Charles's Home Farm on the Duchy of Cornwall Estate and malted to produce Duchy Originals Organic Ale. Further cross-breeding saw Spratt Archer established in 1922. Both strains, and the offspring Standwell, remained the mainstay of the brewing industry until 1953, when Proctor became the most popular type. In terms of yield, Proctor produced some 5.4 more hundredweights per acre than Spratt Archer.

During the 1950s, Wright's Brewery of Perth made much use of locally grown Ymer barley, a Scandinavian cultivar that was rarely seen in England. The name comes from the enormous giant in Norse mythology, named 'Ymer', from whose body the universe is said to have been formed.

The past fifty years have seen the introduction of classical varieties such as Maris Otter, which was first recommended for England and Wales in 1965. It produces a small, plump, even grain that produces exceptionally fine malt. However, the acreage given to Maris Otter is small, as it has been squeezed out by new, higher yielding varieties. It remains popular, however, among brewers of fine traditional ales who have to pay a premium price for it. Maris Otter is also made into malt extract for quality beer kits and extracts for the discerning home brewer.

Golden Promise came on the scene in the 1970s. It is an early ripening variety that is ideal for the Scottish climate and was described as 'the classic malting variety for Scotland'. It was the first cereal in Britain to be given plant breeders' rights.

Today, Optic barley remains popular. It is a late-maturing variety and is harvested in the early autumn and produces good regular malts. However, over the past ten years Crisp Maltings and New Heritage Barley have resurrected Chevallier barley and it is proving popular with breweries at home and abroad, including home brewers. Perhaps we might see some more long-forgotten native barleys emerge in the future.

Barley may be winter or spring sown and will germinate as long as the soil is moist and still retains a degree of warmth. The growth of winter-sown barley is checked by the onset of severe cold conditions, but come warmer springtime weather and growth readily continues. When the barley is harvested in the autumn it contains about 15–20 per cent moisture and a temperature of around 25°C. As such warm moist conditions are favourable for microbial growth, it is essential that the moisture be reduced to at least 12 per cent and the temperature brought down to 15–17°C. To achieve this, the grain was spread out on the granary floor and dried by opening the louvers along the side of the granary so that a gentle current of air flowed across the grain. The bed of barley was turned frequently to ensure that all the kernels dried evenly, reducing the risk of moulds and mildew.

During storage the vitality of barley initially increases, but after a time it slowly starts to decline. Freshly harvested barley also goes through a period of dormancy, a condition that prevents the seed from premature germination. The kernel is also protected with a waxy waterproof coat that prevents the ingress of oxygen and moisture, which would otherwise encourage sprouting. As the grain matures, the waterproof coat slowly dissolves, and by the time favourable 'spring-like' conditions arrive it has all but decomposed and the grain becomes ready for growth.

It is exactly these conditions that the maltster creates to trick the grain into germination and the malt-house ought to be regarded as an artificial field. As Roberts commented, 'there is no process in any known manufacture, in which nature so directly operates, as in malting, and the closer we follow her footsteps, the nearer may we hope to arrive at the desired result'. The busiest period for malting was after Michaelmas ('Micklemas', the festival of St Michael on 29 September) when the weather was neither too warm nor too cold.

Before barley can be used for brewing it first has to be passed through revolving screens to remove all foreign matter, then passed through a winnowing screen to remove dust, and finally finished in a polishing drum. It is now ready for steeping. To ensure that the malt tax was equitable to the maltster and the Excise, strict rules were applied to reduce the likelihood of cheating.

Therefore, before the maltster initiates steeping the grain, he is legally obliged to give the Excise Officer twenty-four hours' notice in writing, with a penalty of £100 should he fail to do so. Also, steeping the barley was restricted between eight in the morning and two in the afternoon, again under a fine of £100 for non-compliance. The maltster was also obliged to keep the grain in the steep fully covered with water for a full forty hours or forfeit £100.[20]

Initially the seeds are screened to remove debris and damaged grains, and are graded into three sizes according to width. This ensures that each seed is evenly wetted to ensure even growth. The grains are now steeped in large cisterns, which have a false perforated bottom just above a conical base. This allows the steep to be drained regularly to allow the seeds to rest and prevent them from becoming waterlogged and drowning, as many would do during a very wet growing season.

The temperature of the steep liquor is typically 47–50°F (8–10°C) and the grain is soaked for 50–80 hours, but the exact time of steeping depends on the variety of barley. In the nineteenth century, Scotch Chevalier and Goldthorpe barleys were steeped for fifty hours; whereas imported Danubian and Odessa barleys were steeped for sixty hours and Smyrmas barley required seventy hours. Moroccan barley was quite course, and as much that could be said for it was that it added roughage to the mash.

The barley is steeped until it absorbs 40–50 per cent moisture, and by doing so it swells almost double in size. During steeping, floating corns, awns and debris are skimmed off. Pre-formed sugars, phosphates and various husk materials, proteins and polyphenols are leached into the liquor and this loss accounts for 0.5–1.5 per cent of the dry weight of the barley. The steep liquor also contains a host of microflora and growth-inhibitory materials, including ethanol that comes from a degree of anaerobic fermentation. A regular change of liquor eliminates such materials and the fresh water introduces essential oxygen for the seedlings.

Traditionally, before the moistened barley was spread out on the malting floor, it was heaped up to into a ruck, or couch, of about 9–29in (23–76cm) high. Eventually a strong rectangular frame was built to a specific size, which allowed more control of the process for malt tax purposes before beer duty was paid on gravity and volume in 1880. The couch is now filled with the barley and levelled off with a piece of wood called a 'strike', and brewers often calculated the volume of malt used in a season by the number of strikes rather than by quarters. The grain must now remain in the couch for at least twenty-six hours.

During couching the biochemical activity of the grain slowly continues and respiration continues to take up oxygen and release carbon dioxide. The first signs of vitality are evident when the seeds start to sprout or 'chit', producing rootlets that are technically called the 'cummings'. During this time, the temperature of the couch starts to rise, which causes the grains to sweat and emit a pungent but pleasing odour.

Germination causes the heat of the couch to rise to about 59–62°F (15–17°C). To regulate the temperature and ensure even growth, the grain is spread out on the malting floor to an initial depth of about 10–16in (25–40cm). Before this is done the Excise Officer gauges the volume in the couch and calculates the malt tax. The 'piece' as the bed of barley is now known is referred to as a 'one-day floor', and on the second day it is called a 'two-day floor' and so on. The aim is now to maintain the temperature of the barley between 48–50°F (9–10°C). To maintain this, the grain is turned regularly and thinned out to not more than 4in (10cm.) This activity also aerates the grain and dissipates CO_2 that would otherwise suffocate the embryo, and prevents the rootlets from becoming entangled.

The piece is now turned regularly with large flat wooden shovels that do not damage the grains. The grain is scooped up and gently strewn in a sprinkling fashion, which releases trapped CO_2 and aerates the embryo and prevents shoots from becoming tangled. As germination proceeds, a great many complex biochemical changes take place, and a host of hydrolytic enzymes will modify the insoluble materials of the foodstore into soluble products that will feed the growing shoots. The embryo also releases a hormone called gibberelin,

which in turn produces gibberellic acid that greatly speeds up synthesis of the enzyme system. To oversimplify this complex activity, we see the enzyme cytase dissolve the cellulose structure of the foodstore. The proteases simplify the proteins, found in the matrix surrounding the starch granules, and in the husk, into peptides and amino acids. This in turn opens up the starchy interior to attack by the amylase enzymes that break it down into a range of sugars to feed the growing shoots. Phytase frees up soluble phosphorus products that create a degree of acidity and lipases simplify the natural oils, or lipids, into a range of fatty acids, which will support respiration. The extent to which this process is allowed to continue is referred to as 'modification'.

In nature this process would continue until all the goodness in the foodstore was utilised by the growing shoots so that they become well established and the plant can then start to draw its energy from the sun and soil. However, the maltster only allows germination to proceed to a point where sufficient modification takes place and the interior of the kernel is in a friable state. By doing so he preserves the maximum amount of starch that the brewer requires to convert into sugars and eventually alcohol. The proteins, too, are only digested to a point where they are reduced to a level where sufficient simpler products, such as peptides and amino acids, are available for yeast nutrition. The balance of protein remaining should not cause haze in the finished product but provide sufficient protein in the form of polypeptides to satisfy palate fullness and head retention.

Over the next few days, the barley is regularly turned to maintain an even temperature. Sometimes large wooden rakes are used instead of shovels to achieve the same end, but if the heat of the piece has to be rapidly reduced it is turned with a wooden plough that will turn over much larger quantities very quickly. Thickening or thinning the piece also controls the temperature so that heat is retained or lost respectively. The malthouse louvers are opened or closed as required to increase or decrease the airflow over the piece, and such ventilation is necessary to dissipate heat and moisture and so control the temperature of the grain. The ventilation has to be closely controlled, as too much draught over the piece will affect premature withering of the shoots.

The physical appearance of the corns will tell the maltster just how well germination is proceeding. During growth the acrospire (coleoptile) grows slowly, just visible under the husk, and a number of small rootlets appear from the base of the seed. The number of rootlets indicates the degree of modification that is taking place, and the moisture level of the piece also has an influence on the amount of root formation. If the moisture level of the piece is too high and too much warmth accompanies this, the growth of the rootlets becomes excessive at the expense of acrospire growth, which results in excessive depletion of starch in the foodstore, resulting in a loss of extract for the brewer. Ideally the rootlets should be short and bushy and no longer than one centimetre, and the maltster has to control as best he can the malting conditions to ensure that the growth of the acrospire and modification keep pace with root-formation. It is also important that the rootlets do not dry up, and an early indication of this is that they tend to lose their turgid appearance. Should this happen, the piece will require to be wetted by sprinkling it with water that might contain some bisulphate of lime to check microbial growth.

The length of the acrospire dictates the degree of modification. After ten to fourteen days on the floor, the acrospire will be at three-quarters the length of the corn and is fully modified. The 'green malt' now has to be prepared for kilning and the piece is now left unturned for the next twenty-four hours. During this period the louvers are kept tightly shut so that no ventilation occurs, which results in a build-up of CO_2 that suffocates the embryo and arrests germination. During this time the piece collects heat and loses moisture, causing the rootlets to wither.

The Strae kiln.

Primitive malting saw the malt simple dried in the sun or in earthenware pots over a smouldering fire. Improvements saw the development of the 'strae-kiln' (Straw-kiln), which consisted of a small cavern dug out in the side of a hillock that was covered with branches and straw with an opening at the rear. The grain was placed over the straw roof and a small fire of straw, peat, turf and whin was used to fire the kiln, which was lit at the front and as the heat from the fire was drawn to the rear opening it rose up through the bed of grain and dried it. Eventually the strae kiln gave way to the bee-hive-shaped stone kilns that worked on the same principle, and abandoned examples can still be found in the north of Scotland and the Western Isles. The malt dried by this method would have remained fairly pale but would also acquire a smoky flavour. Pale malts are kilned to just wither the growing shoots and heat sensitive proteolytic enzymes, but do not destroy the important amylases that are required during mashing. The exact temperature and time in the kiln, however, is dependent on the type of malt being produced and was very much an empirical process.

Despite the fact that the smokiness of the malt would dissipate considerably during storage, the flavour would linger in the brew and affect the head of those who were not used to drinking it. Consequently, this led to the search for better methods of drying the grain without smokiness. The breakthrough came in England on 23 July 1638, when Nicholas Halse brought out a patent, number 85, of a design for a drying kiln that used seacoal turf and other fuels, which did not smoke the malt.[37]

With the introduction of coke circa 1680, the kilning process became much more controlled. Eighteen years later, on 28 November 1698, J. Gronan and T. Reeve took out a patent to dry malt on iron, or tinned iron, and malt was dried without any contact with smoke. This method also used 50 per cent less fuel than previously.[36]

Many attempts were made to improve upon roasting techniques and the quantum leap came in 1817, when Daniel Wheeler patented his 'new and improved method of Drying and Preparation of Malt'. Wheeler's drum roasting device was made of thin iron that revolved slowly over a fierce fire. The intense direct heat of 360–400°F (180–204°C) dried and then roasted the malt until the desired degree of colour was obtained. To prevent carbonisation and charring of the grain, internal water sprays would douse and cool the malt, thereby arresting the roasting. Now, for the first time, the maltster could accurately control the exact degree of colour and changes that took place within the grain without charring taking place. Scottish maltsters and brewers capitalised on this device and roasted the floaters from the steep and slack barley, which was then used in porter and stout brewing.

To protect his interests, Wheeler took out a patent on his invention and roasted malt was referred to as 'patent malt' or 'patent black malt'. Patent malt became the principal flavouring and colorant in porter beer, and in Ireland it became known as porter malt. From this time, we see the introduction of other coloured malts such as chocolate malt, amber malt, crystal malt and roasted barley, which are still in vogue today. However, by the turn of the nineteenth century Scottish brewers were using pale malt for Scotch Pale Ale and India beers and pale malt, amber malt, brown malt and patent black malt were used in making porter and stout.

Originally and prior to brewing, the grain would have been crushed on a flat or slightly concave stone by a round stone or stone rolling pin. Later, we see the introduction of the 'quern' that consisted of two circular flat stones, the lower one with grooves running out from the centre. The top stone had a wooden handle and a central hole through which the grain was fed. As the top stone was turned the ground meal, oats or barley, slowly migrated through the grooves to the periphery, where it was collected. The quern remained in use in Orkney and Shetland until the turn of the nineteenth century. Later, horse-drawn mills, water mills and windmills were constructed and the grain was crushed between two revolving stones made from local sandstone or millstone grit, typically found in Yorkshire, and later 'buhr', a very hard stone imported from France.

The disadvantage of millstones was that crushing was very irregular, which meant that in many cases the grain was either poorly crushed or excessively crushed. In the former this left too much husk and not enough flour for conversion into sugars that would eventually be converted into alcohol. If the grain was crushed too fine, the excessive quantity of flour quickly formed a paste in the mash tun, which resulted in a set mash and low yield.

During the 1840s, Scottish pale malt was typically kiln-dried at 70°F (21°C) to reduce the moisture content before final curing, and at this stage the malt is said to be 'hand dry'. The thickness of the piece largely dictated drying time and if it was about 7in (177mm) thick, kilning might last for up to 80–90 hours. Should the piece be thinner at about 5in (127mm), the drying time was about 60–70 hours, and in both cases, the final curing of pale malt took place at 140°F (60°C).

Slowly, improvements in kilning technology continued, and by the middle of the nineteenth century we see the introduction of indirect heated double-floored kilns. The double-floored kiln was a major advance in the drying and curing of malt, which apart from being more efficient cut the kilning time in half. In the double-floored kiln the green malt might spend up to 60–72 hours in the upper chamber, being regularly turned to ensure even drying under a moderate heat. Thereafter, the still moist green malt was dried at 158°F (70°C), which restricted melanoidin formation that would darken the wort. The now pale malt is dropped to the hotter lower chamber for the final curing that might take as little as thirty-six hours.

Amber malt was cured at 150–155°F (65–68°C) and was either finished in the kiln or Wheeler's roasting cylinder to achieve a pale amber hue retaining diastatic activity. Today, amber malt is cured at 280–300°F (138–149°C) acquiring a colour of 35–100 EBC° and a warm dry biscuit flavour. It may be diastatic or non-diastatic. Brown malt, which is also called 'blown' malt, followed a different route and after germination it was quickly conveyed to the drying kiln, where it was spread out very thinly and partially dried under a moderate heat. Thereafter, the heat was dramatically increased with a roaring fire of hardwood battens that produced a somewhat empyreumatic flavour.[28] At Steel and Coulson's Greenhead Brewery, Glasgow, blown malt for stout brewing was dried at a high temperature by using birchwood.

Final curing at 155–160°F (68–71°C) caused the still moist malt to rapidly swell up by some 25 per cent and became popped or blown. Brown malt is now cured at 350°F (177°) producing a colour of 200–400 EBC°. An old method of preparing barley was to wet it and then pass it through a bed of red-hot sand that effected a crude form of torrification, which caused the grain to swell up and 'pop' and acquire a nutty flavour. Today, this is achieved by micronisation.

After the malt has been cured, the next step is to remove the cummings, which are rich in protein and therefore a valuable source of pig and cattle feed. Before the introduction of mechanical sieving devices, the cummings were removed by workmen trampling over the piece wearing heavy boots, a practice that must surely have damaged some of the grains. In the mid-seventeenth century, it was common for Highland women to trample malt in a wooden tub with their feet. Finally, the grain was passed through a fan-driven winnowing machine.

By the end of the nineteenth century, Scottish brewers were importing six-rowed barley from abroad that inevitably had higher nitrogen (protein) content than indigenous barley.

A consequence of this was that the malt required longer kilning heats to break down the nitrogenous materials, and longer coppering to induce a greater hot break of the proteins and achieve clarity and stability of the brew. The longer boiling also increased the colour of the wort due to formation of colour precursors called melanoidins.

When we consider the low kilning heats in the 1840s, the colour of pale malt must have fairly light, around 3–4 EBC°. By the late nineteenth century, the final kilning heats were about 195–205°F (91–96°C), which increased the colour, and it is most likely from this period that the colour of Scottish malts crept up to 7–9 EBC°, giving pale ales of the late nineteenth and early twentieth centuries a fuller character and amber hue. High-dried malt and imported barleys might also spend longer in the kiln to improve flavour.

The first strong wort from the mash tun would be the darkest and contain the maximum amount of melanoidin colour precursors. Consequently, after coppering for 1½–2 hours the colour of bitter wort for Scotch Ale and strong Export beers would be between amber and nut-brown. The second wort drawn off for table beer would be lighter in colour precursors and so the beer would be pale amber. Should a third wort be drawn off for small beer, it would be paler, about the colour of straw.

After the Union of the Crowns in 1603, Scotland retained its own parliament, and in 1707, under the Act of Union, the Scottish parliament was dissolved and Scotland became part of the United Kingdom. In general, the Scots were opposed to the union with England, and to sweeten the pill they were offered many concessions. One of these was that the English Malt Tax of 6*d* per bushel was not to be applied in Scotland until after the War of the Spanish Succession, or for a period of seven years after the date of the union. The Spanish War of Succession ended in 1713, and in direct defiance of the treaty the government wasted no time in levying the tax on malt on the Scots. This act caused a huge outrage north of the border, and the Scottish nobility sitting in the House of Lords was so disaffected that it almost led to the dissolution of the Union.[19]

Some of the arguments against the malt tax were that it would increase the price of the ale on which the population, particularly the poor, relied for sustenance. Prior to this time, the Scots paid no tax on the ingredients for brewing beer, which was known in Glasgow as 'the poor man's wine'. It was also argued, quite correctly, that Scots malt was inferior to English malt and that it sold at a lesser price. However, the malt tax cannot be taken in isolation as the main focus of discontent for there were other taxes on such goods as linen, soap, beer and salt, which were all taking their toll on the Scottish economy.

In order to mitigate the excise on malt, the Scots proposed that it should be reduced to 3*d* per bushel, but this was rejected and the full tax was levied. This decision unleashed a wave of anger and riots broke out in all the major Scottish cities, particularly Glasgow, whose MP, Duncan Campbell, who voted for the Bill, had the mob attack his Shawfield Mansion and two companies of troops were brought in to quell the riot. In the ensuing chaos nine people were killed and sixteen wounded.[19] Such was the furore over the Shawfield Riots that the maltsters largely ignored the Malt Tax and it was never wholly enforced.

By 1724, the government needed to raise £20,000 from the Scottish economy, and this was to be gained by a malt tax of 6*d* per bushel. The Scots were also to be deprived of the bounty of exporting grain to England, and despite a huge uproar by the gentry and the Jacobites, the malt tax was introduced on 23 June 1725. Such was the angry response by the public that the Excise Officers had to take flight!

By the end of 1725, the 6*d* per bushel was rescinded and the malt tax reduced to 3*d* per bushel. During the reign of George II (1727–60) the malt tax in Scotland was raised to 3/11*d* and 5/20ths of a penny per boll. During the reign of

George III in 1802, it was raised to 10/- and 15/20ths of a penny per boll. In 1803, it was raised to £1 and 2/- and 15/20ths of a penny per boll.

The malt tax was only levied on the common brewers, not private or domestic brewers. However, householders did not escape the clutches of the Exciseman, for instead of paying an annual malt tax, each household was obliged to pay a compounded tax of 7/6*d* per head of the household. This was equal to the tax on ten bushels of malt, which was considered an average amount of malt that the typical family would consume in a year.

In 1830, The Duke of Wellington's Beerhouse Act repealed the duty on beer, although the tax on hops remained until 1862 and the malt tax remained on the statute books until 1880. However, the domestic brewer was not to escape the taxman, and those who wished to brew at home for their own consumption were obliged to apply for an annual home brewer's licence. The licence fee was determined by the rateable value of one's premises, and if the annual valuation was less than £8, no licence was required. However, if the rateable value was over £8 and up to £15, a licence was required but the householder was not charged any duty. With the passage of time the rating system became archaic and the legislation was not amended, although it remained on the Statute Book, and by 1963 the licence fee was levied at 5*s*. In reality, nobody bothered to apply for a licence to brew, and as the cost involved in trying to collect it far outweighed the revenue that might be obtained the Chancellor, Reginald Maudling, decided to repeal the legislation in his budget of 1963.

Looking back in time, we can see that a variety of cereals were used in brewing to augment the starches in barley. When unmalted cereals are used in brewing, they are referred to as 'adjuncts', that is to say, something joined to another but not essentially part of it. For example, should the brewer add a quantity of raw barley to his mash tun, it is called a malt adjunct, although the purists amongst us usually refer to adjuncts as adulterants! However, this is largely based on ignorance and misconception. This bias is based on the fact that some countries banned adjuncts outright or limit their use in the mistaken belief that only all-malt can produce good beer. Whilst there is no doubt that an all-malt brew has an excellent 'quality of palate', much depends on the quality of the barley for malting, and as British brewers traditionally imported foreign barleys the overall quality of the malt grist and wort was not always up to scratch.

The theory behind the all-malt crusade lies deep in history, particular Bavaria, where, in 1516, Duke Wilhelm IV introduced the Reinheitsgebot; the so-called purity law that the traditionalists believe stated that only malt, hops, yeast and water could be used for brewing beer. However, due to research by Ian Hornsey, we now know the Reinheitsgebot does not even mention malt or indeed yeast, which was still a mysterious ingredient until the late nineteenth century! What was actually written was that in his 'towns, market places and on throughout the country… that beer should only be brewed from water, barley and hops'.[29] Consequently, the law only applied to towns and not, as widely believed, the whole of Bavaria. In reality, the purity law was designed to outlaw the importation of foreign cereals, so that the duke could develop the brewing industry and increase taxes to get rid of the debt that he had built up due to military campaigns. After Germany became a unified country in 1871, the Reinheitsgebot became law throughout the country.

In 1625, we see similar protectionist measures in Scotland when parliament passed a law that banned 'the hamebringing of foreyne beir'. This act was to prevent the importation of English and foreign beer that was a threat to domestic farmers and brewers, and in 1627, imported ales were taxed £6 per tun. In the UK, adjuncts were banned in 1802 and only malt and hops were legally allowed in brewing. This Act outlawed the use of cheaper cereals that saw financial benefits for the Chancellor of the Exchequer.

In the 1850s, the government introduced smooth roller mills that would satisfactorily crush malt but not unmalted cereals, and so Customs could easily catch cheats. Technically, too, poorly crushed grains would result in poor extract recovery and haze and would be uneconomical. This state of affairs remained in force until 1880, when Gladstone repealed the malt and sugar tax and levied duty on wort gravity and volume, which meant that brewers were now free to acquire fermentable extract from a variety of ingredients.

Not everyone agreed with the Free Mash-Tun Act, and all-malt brewers complained that brewers who used cheaper ingredients made larger profits from inferior ingredients. In 1885, Sir Cuthbert Quilter introduced a Pure Beer Bill in parliament, arguing that 'beer' meant a brew made from malt, hops, water and yeast, and that cereal adjuncts and sugar should be banned. By 1899 a Parliamentary Committee had looked into the issue, and no doubt they came under pressure from the powerful sections of the brewing industry and decided on the status quo. However, despite the 'Free Mash-Tun Act' there was no widespread abuse of adjuncts, and in 1899, the 'glorious year of the maltster', a typical English brewer's grist consisted of 85 per cent malt, 5 per cent mash tun adjuncts and 10 per cent copper sugars, whilst Scottish brewers used 94 per cent malt and 6 per cent copper sugars.

The Act also prompted E.S. Beaven, who was a pioneer on pure line barleys, particularly Plumage Archer, to comment that the malt tax was 'injuriously affected the interests of the British barley grower, mainly by encouraging the use of cheaper foreign barley for malting'. However, it should not be overlooked that the use of adjuncts was in many cases technically desirable, and due to the irregularity of the malts on offer around the turn of the century the Customs and Excise sanctioned the use of diastatic malt extracts in the mash tun in 1906 to ensure a good quality of wort and beer. In twentieth-century France, adjuncts were limited to 15 per cent of the total materials in order to encourage local agriculture.[28]

The commonest mash tun adjuncts used in brewing are maize, rice, wheat, barley, rye and oats. Just how much to use and what pre-brewing treatment they might require is taken into financial and technical consideration. Maize, for example, has to be harvested and the kernels removed. Next, its oily embryo and lipids are removed, as they will have a deleterious effect on beer quality, and are pre-cooked to gelatinize its starches so that it is readily digested in the mash tun and finally passed through heated rollers to produce corn flakes.

Technically, flaked maize is useful for diluting the nitrogen levels in malt grist as its proteins are not acted upon by the proteolytic enzymes in malt and consequently there is an overall dilution of troublesome proteins. Should the proteins be on the high side, it can cause a protein haze, particularly in high gravity beers, and also due to the long maturation times the microbial stability of the brew might also be affected. The enzymic content of typical two-rowed mash could adequately cope with 15 per cent maize. However, as some brewers used as much as 60 per cent six-rowed barley, the mash required 40 per cent flaked maize to dilute it. As six-rowed barley has a higher enzymic content the mash could cope with the larger amount of flaked maize.

Flaked rice has more use in lager beer and flaked wheat is primarily used to aid head retention due to the polysaccharides, particularly pentosans sugars, that are not fermentable by yeast. Flaked barley, or more commonly micronized barley, finds more use in stouts due to its grainy nuance. Flaked oats are used in some beers such as Oat Malt Stout, and in lesser amounts for flavour and texture in other stout and beer. Oats were pressed into service during the Second World War due to a shortage of barley malt, but quickly went out of favour when brewing restrictions ended after 1945. The problem with oats is that they have high lipid and protein levels that affect head retention, although they have a high fibrous husk that benefits good runnings of worts.

Oats were also used to make two types of sowans ('so'anz'):

1. A flummery made from the farina (starch) remaining in the husks of oats. The 'sowan-seeds' were steeped in a sowens-bowie and allowed to ferment for several days, before straining off the liquor through a sowans sieve to retrieve the sowan paste from the vessel. It was often supped on its own or when cold mixed and cooked with oatmeal to make sowan-porridge. On Christmas Eve sowans formed part of the fair along with bread, cheese and ale. The practice of 'sowening' was also carried out when sowans paste was smeared on neighbours' doors for luck. Sowans paste was also used as a weaver's paste.

2. The mildly alcoholic liquor strained from the sowans was supped as a thirst-quenching drink at harvest time. Another refreshing harvest drink was 'Blenshaw', which was made by putting a teaspoonful of oatmeal in a glass with a teaspoonful of sugar. To this was added a gill of milk that was stirred until quite creamy, and then the glass was topped up with boiling water. The drink was flavoured with grated nutmeg and drunk when cool.

THE VICTORIAN BREWERY AND PUBLIC HOUSE

'Among the achievements of the latter half of the present century, few have been fraught with more beneficial consequences than the practical application of the deductions of science to manufacturing applications. Nearly every important industry has passed from the empirical to the scientific age.'

Walter J. Sykes, *The Principles and Practices of Brewing*, 1897

Many of Scotland's breweries built between 1881 and 1901 were designed by the renowned Edinburgh architect Peter Lyle Henderson. His work included the Slatefield Brewery, Glasgow, in 1881; The Crown Brewery, Glasgow, 1882; the Sidegate Brewery, Haddington, 1883; the Prestonpans Brewery, 1884; the Edinburgh & Leith Brewery, 1888; The Craigmillar Brewery,1888; The Anchor Brewery, Glasgow, 1889; Deuchar's Brewery, Duddingston, 1894; the Home Brewery, Glasgow, 1895; the North British Brewery, Duddingston, 1896; the Thornbush Brewery and Maltings, Inverness, 1897; Aitken's Brewery, Falkirk, 1900; and the Pentland Brewery, Duddingston, 1901. Two of his outstanding works were Ballingall's Park Brewery, Dundee, in 1880–81, which Barnard described as 'This magnificent brewery, built entirely of pressed red bricks with white facings with a Grecian border that ornaments the upper portions of the buildings, relieving the heaviness of the lofty structure.' The other was the St Leonards Brewery, Edinburgh, 1889–90, that was built for George McKay with rubble masonry faced with red ashlar in the traditional Scottish Baronial style.

Henderson also designed new maltings at the Croft-an-Righ Brewery; new cellars and tun room for the Edinburgh & Leith Brewery; and new stables for John Fowler & Co. Prestonpans, plus many public houses. Is it any wonder then that he became known as 'the brewer's architect'?

A fairly typical Victorian brewery was built on the gravitational system that allowed each stage of the process to descend to the next by gravity, which saved on floor space and the need for pumps to move the brew on to the next stage. Pumps were also a source of infections and consequently demanded scrupulous and time-consuming cleaning. The main disadvantage of a tower brewery is that it does not allow for the extension of the brewery as trade increases and demands more plant. It also means more 'leg-work' for the brewer and staff, as they regularly move up and down an external stairway checking on each phase of brewing. However, by the 1880s lifts connecting all floors became common.

Below a brewery was the all-important well that supplied the 'liquor' for malting, mashing, coppering, cooling and cleaning. Historically, brewers simply used the liquor straight from the well, which usually had a cool temperature of about 50°F (10°C) and was biologically pure. It was simply an observation that brewers recognised that the liquor in certain localities was better suited to a specific type of beer, and Burton upon Trent with its gypseous water was well known for its pale ales; London and Dublin supporting carbonates became renowned for porter and stout; and Edinburgh with its hard water drawn from the so-called 'Charmed Circle', a structural trough of Old Red Sandstone below Arthur's Seat, was famous for its full-flavoured pale ales.

However, with the advancement of science in the late nineteenth century, brewers developed the means of treating the liquor as necessary to achieve a mineral balance suited to the type of beer being brewed, and could brew a range of pale ale, porter, dry and sweet stouts and mild ale from one liquor source. In general, sulphate liquors are better suited to pale ales as they influence a dry palate, and stouts benefit from chlorides that act as flavour enhancers, coaxing out the luscious flavours from the roasted malts. Whilst the sulphate/chloride ratio in typical English pale ale is 2:1, which suits their characteristic bitterness, Scottish pale ales benefit from a ratio of 3:2 that complements their fuller flavour and malt sweetness. The well water was pumped to the highest point of the brewery and was stored in wooden lead-lined or cast-iron tanks, and before brewing commenced it was run down into the well-insulated hot liquor tank and heated by steam injection to about 176°F (80°C) from the exhaust of the coppers below. Its heat was gauged by a thermometer that had by now come into regular use.

Prior to mashing, the quantity of malt has to be worked out to achieve the required gravity of the beer. This calculation is based on brewer's pounds per quarter, a quarter being 336lb of malt. For example, if we wish to brew 100 gallons of beer with a gravity of 1.055, we subtract 1.000, which leaves 55 and we multiply this by 0.36, which equals one barrel of 36 gallons, and we have 19.8 brewer's pounds. A hundred barrels multiplied by 19.8 gives us 1,980lbs, the quantity of malt required. If we assume that the average yield from one quarter of malt equals 86 brewer's lbs, and we divide 1,980 by 86, we require 23 quarters of malt to produce a gravity of 55. The Victorians also calculated the weight of malt by the bushel that weighs 42lb, and so the number of bushels required is 23 qtrs x 336lb / 42 = 184 bushels.

Before mashing, the malt is screened through a sieve to remove foreign bodies such as nails and small stones. The malt was also checked for its moisture content, which should be below 3 per cent, and should it be higher it was termed as 'slack'. As slack malt weighs more than dry malt, the brewer's calculations will be inaccurate. Before the introduction of moisture meters, slack malt was detected by plunging one's hand into the sack to detect clamminess, and if the malt was slack some of the kernels might stick to the hand when it was withdrawn. The brewer might also chew a few grains to check that the interior is crisp, and should it be soft this indicates slackness and the batch rejected.

The malt is now lightly crushed between a pair of smooth revolving rollers of steel or cast iron. The gap between the rollers can be set with utmost precision to produce about 10 per cent flour, 70 per cent fine grits and 20 per cent course grits, and might be sieved and graded to achieve this end. This degree of crushing is essential to ensure good mashing efficiency, good running of wort, and recovery of extract. The mills are housed in cabinets that retain the malt dust, which, if ignited by the sparks given off by a nail or flint that has evaded the pre-sieving process, can cause an explosion and fire. To avoid this possibility, some sieves were fitted with magnets to capture any of the metal fragments that are frequently found in malt.

Next, the malt is conveyed to the grist case, which is situated immediately above the mash tun, by a Jacob's ladder, which is a continuous leather belt fitted with light metallic buckets that scoop up the crushed malt and convey it to the grist case. The Jacob's ladder takes its name from Jacob's Biblical dream where he saw angels ascending and descending a stairway to Heaven, and it is enclosed within a wooden casing. Later, in some breweries, the Jacob's ladder was replaced by an elevator or screw conveyor.

Traditionally, the mash tun was made of indigenous oak slightly tapered inwards, so that the iron hoops could be well driven to clamp the staves together, rendering the vessel watertight. Eventually mash tuns became copper-lined, a process that made cleaning easier and extended their lifespan considerably. Fowler's of Prestonpans were one of the first breweries to instal cast-iron mash tuns. The base of the mash tun is covered with perforated gun metal or cast-iron plates that would allow the sweet wort to drain. When mashing, the hot liquor at about 185°F (85°C) is let down into the mash tun, and as it warms up the tun the heat drops to that

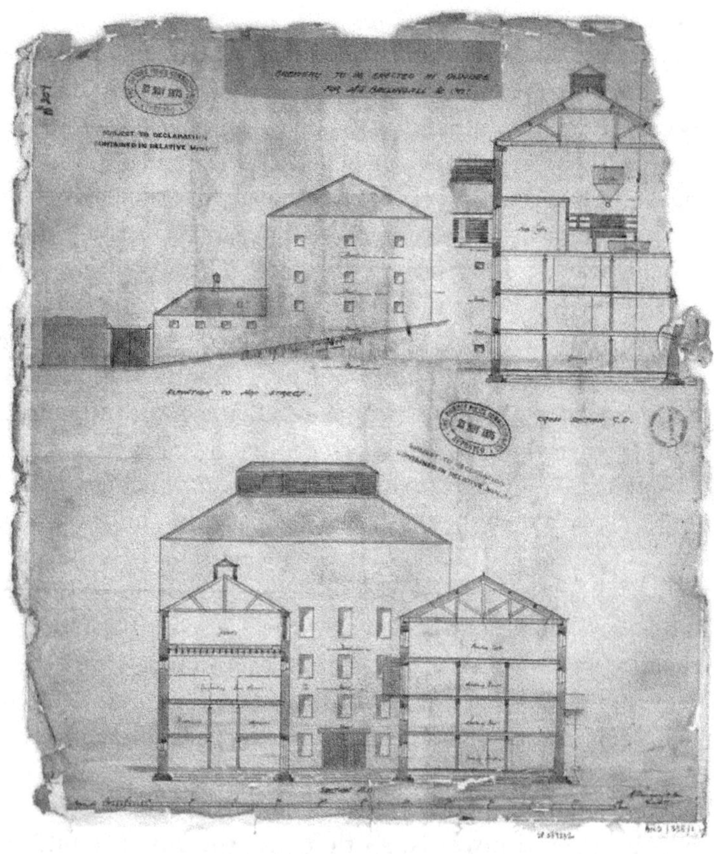

Plans for Ballingall's New Park Brewery, 1875.

desired and the grist doughed in. The mash is now manually and vigorously roused in with oars and rakes to ensure that all balls and lumps of malt flour are broken up to give full contact to the hot liquor, which will ensure a successful mash. The process takes about fifty minutes, and when completed the surface of the mash is covered with a bushel of dry malt to preserve the heat. The mash tun is now covered and left to stand for 2–3 hours to fully saccharify.

By the 1880s, steam-heated cast-iron mash tuns were in vogue. Initially warmed up by steam injection into the insulated casing, the hot liquor then enters a Steel's external masher, and at the same time the valve on the grist case is opened to allow both materials to intimately mix, before falling into the mash tun. Once in the mash tun, revolving Anderson rakes finally mixed the mash into a fine porridge with a typical initial heat of 158°F (70°C). It is now called the 'goods'. The mash is now covered and left to saccharify, and during this time very complex biological activity takes place and host of amolytic enzymes slowly transform the malt flour into a range of sugars, typically 75 per cent fermentable maltose and 25 per cent unfermentable dextrin. The balance of such sugars is manipulated by the brewer's choice of initial mash heats, and if slightly below 150°F (65.5°C) more maltose is produced, and if slightly above more dextrin is created. This has important consequences for the type of beer being produced. In Robert's day, liquor heats were typically high, say about 180°F (82°C) to 190°F (87°C), but much depended on the temperature of the atmosphere and the crushed malt, and judgement had to be made to achieve the best saccharification of the mash, which was about 158°F (70°C). This high heat produced lots of dextrin, some of which sustained the yeast during up to a year's maturation and provided the characteristic full-bodied sweet characteristic in old Scotch Ales.

As the mash heat slowly falls, this was corrected by underletting, whereby a quantity of hot liquor was fed into the mash tun underneath its perforated false bottom or by a clever invention, which had been in use since 1865, of hollow revolving perforated rakes that would inject steam into the mash and raise its heat. After 2–3 hours the sweet wort produced now has to be drawn off. This was done by 'setting taps', the process of draining and spairging (sparging) that is necessary to wash out the absorbed wort from the goods to ensure maximum recovery of extract. Roberts considered that he had a satisfactory mash heat if the runnings from the mash tun were in the region of 147°F (64°C) to 150°F (66.6°C).

The sparger consists of two perforated arms, or wings, rotating on a central axis that delivers a spray of hot liquor at a much higher temperature than that of the goods, usually about 190°F (87.7°C). The taps on the mash tun are now partially slacked or opened in sequence to ensure an even draining, so that the goods settle down evenly without creating a fissure that would allow too much sparge liquor to run through the crack, resulting in low extract recovery. When the wort is flowing uninterruptedly the taps are fully opened, and as soon as the wort drains just below the surface of the goods, sparging commences. The sparging technique was known as 'fly-sparging', a term first used by Levesque in his *Art of Brewing* in 1853, whereby a balance was achieved between the liquor falling on the surface of the goods and the wort running from the taps. This ensured that the goods remained buoyant and floated just above the false bottom, obtaining good extract recovery. The brewer now collects the first third of the sweet wort that is required for high gravity ales such as No.1 Scotch Ale or Seven, Eight, Ten, Twelve and Fifteen Guinea Ales, or 100/- to 160/- Ales. The second runnings were used for beers of lower gravity and the last dregs produced small beer.

The next stage is 'coppering', which is necessary to condense the wort to the required gravity, and a consequence is that it is sterilised and no further enzyme activity takes place, so the ratio of dextrin and maltose is fixed. Quality hops are now added to infuse the brew with their bitter spicy flavoursome properties and preservative resins, which, in conjunction with the balance of sugar obtained from the mash tun, produce the character of the brew. Only the choicest hops were added for high-quality ales, and the time of coppering was limited to preserve the delicate flavour and aromatic principles of the hop. Lesser-quality ales might be infused with a blend of the spent hops perked up with some old or new hops. During coppering the high-gravity ales acquired a degree of caramelisation, and in conjunction with residual sweetness added to the fullness of palate in Scotch Ale.

After coppering is complete, the spent hops need to be strained out, and if the copper did not have an internal strainer, then a hop back (called a 'dish') was required. The hop back could be made of wood or iron, and it too was fitted with straining plates to filter out the hops. As the hops settled down on the straining plates, they form a natural sieve that retains the proteinaceous debris from coppering called the 'hot-break'. The hop back might also be fitted with a sparger to rinse out the last dregs of valuable extract, and some brewers added a charge of fresh hops to the hop back, extracting further aromatics from the essential oils.

After coppering, it was necessary to cool the wort as quickly as possible to a pitching heat for the yeast that was typically 50°F (10°C). The early coolers were large shallow wooden vessels about 6–8in (15–20cm) in depth so that the wort readily gave up its heat to the atmosphere. They were usually situated at the top of the brewery with open louvers that provided a constant cool draught, and later models where lined with copper. A brewery might have up to six coolers positioned at

The open cooler at the Half Moon Brewery, Bruges.

different heights, and after a short period in the upper one the wort was run down into the other vessels with a depth of only about one inch. This quickly reduced the temperature, also assisted by a cooling draught from the louvres that ran along the side of the building, although some breweries employed 'fanners' that consisted of two flat blades of metal attached at right angles to a vertical axis that was driven mechanically from below and blew a constant draught off the surface of the wort.

As Scottish brewers usually brewed between October and April, the cold weather ensured that the wort cooled quickly within 6–8 hours, and aerial contaminations were rare as the yeast quickly multiplied and overwhelmed competing bacteria. An early primitive form of artificial cooling that was still in force in Robert's day consisted of a spiral metal pipe that was coiled inside a large vessel of cold well water and connected to the hop back. As the wort was run from the hop back through the coil it lost its heat, from about 180°F (82°C) to 50°F

(10°C), before it dropped into the squares, picking up a degree of aeration as it did so and the yeast was roused in. Cast-iron coolers started to appear in Edinburgh breweries early in the nineteenth century, and these were very efficient.

As early as 1862 we see the invention by Dr Kirk of the air machine, a compressed-air refrigerator that became widely used in ice-making.[29] In 1881, Ballingall's of Dundee installed two Stanley-Reece ammonia ice-making machines in the new Park Brewery that used up to 30,000 gallons of water daily, and these were made by Pontifex & Wood of London. Not only did this chill the water supply to 38°F (3°C) for the open horizontal refrigerators, but it also passed through pipework surrounding the fermentation and flattening rooms and beer cellars, which meant that brewing could take place throughout the year rather than being restricted to the cold months from October to April.

The fermentation squares were typically made of oak or fir, but in the case of Fowler's Prestonpans Brewery they were made of slate that was later lined with copper, and held up to sixty barrels. Fir required seasoning with scalding hot water, followed by a coat of chloride of lime. After twenty-four hours the vat is washed out with diluted hydrochloric acid, followed by being rinsed out with hot water, and finally the vat is coated with bisulphate of lime to neutralise the chlorine. American cedar was infinitely superior to fir, as it did not require seasoning and after a good scrub out with hot water it was ready for use.[59] Unlike the mash tun that had upright staves, the squares consisted of level planks planed smooth and bolted tightly together, so that when the square is filled with beer the slight swelling of the wet timber renders them absolutely beer-tight.

The yeast was usually pitched at 50°F, although 45–46°F was not uncommon. The progress of fermentation is noticeable after some 8–12 hours, when the quiescent surface of the wort is covered with a light froth that gradually changes into 'cauliflower' heads, that evolve into thick curly foam forming little rocky peaks. When this stage is reached, the yeast crop is roused back into the beer to ensure a satisfactory attenuation. Without a saccharometer, the old brewer could judge just what stage the fermentation was at by the appearance of the yeast head. He might also simply dip his finger into the wort and taste it, and the degree of sweetness would tell him the degree of attenuation.

The fermentation profile was quite cool at 50–60°F (10–16°C) and lasted for up to twenty-one days. When fermentation is coming to an end, the yeast rises to the top of the brew, forming the 'closed head' that offers the brew protection from oxidation and airborne bugs. The brew is now skimmed and dropped to the 'flattening squares' below for cleansing, where some of the yeast deposits form another closed head so that the beer is relatively clean of yeast. After a short rest the brew is skimmed and racked into hogsheads. Each cask is dry hopped with the choicest aromatic Kent Goldings, which will over a period of three or more weeks impregnate the beer with a floral aroma. Depending on the type of beer being brewed, it might be stored in the bitter beer cellar or the sweet beer cellar.

After a period of maturation, the brew was considered to be ripe and mellow, and it was casked or bottled ready for sale. Draught shilling ales for the local and family trade were usually racked into pins, firkins or kilderkins. Beer for bottling was always racked into hogsheads and designated under the guinea terminology. Casks were made of Baltic oak, and the best timber came from Stettin, Memel and Danzig. Casks were a huge financial outlay for a brewery, and to keep track of where they were each cask was stamped with the brewery name and given a serial number that was logged on dispatch and recorded on return. Casks that went astray in the home market were bad enough, but if the importers in foreign markets failed to return a cask, usually hogsheads, then the financial loss was considerable. Casks returning from London might be unheaded and filled with hops, and from further afield with non-perishable goods.

Casks returning to the brewery were unheaded and scrubbed out with hot water containing bisulphite of lime to keep them 'sweet', then stored in the cask yard to benefit from a good airing. Prior to reuse they were re-headed and steam cleaned and taken to the racking cellar. The cellarman might also carry out the 'snifter test', in which he simply smells the cask for hints of contamination, and if not satisfied that the cask is 'sweet' it undergoes another rigorous cleaning. Unwashed and unheaded casks that became polluted with rainwater invariably became rancid and were known as 'stinkers', leading to their destruction.

With the cottage system in olden times, barrels had a large square bung hole so that the brewer could get his arm inside to clean the cask. The cask was finally given a 'heather rinse' to keep it sweet.

The cooperage was a very important department, not only for making casks, but also care and maintenance of wooden mash tuns and fermenting and flattening squares. The cooper was a skilled artisan who underwent a seven-year apprenticeship, and it was not uncommon for son to follow father into the trade. At the turn of the century a cooper's wage was 30/- per week, on par with the brewery foreman and mechanics, as opposed to the general brewery labourer earning 20/- a week.

A strong cask was made from the best Crown Memel oak, which is relatively free from knots and has low tannin content. After being cut to size, the staves are given a lengthy soak to leach out further tannins, and then stacked in the open to season. When required, the cooper selects the staves, and using backing and hollowing knives gives each one the right amount of taper and hollow by eye so that the stave is slightly bow-shaped. Once all the staves have been prepared, they are fitted into an end hoop that holds them together and then a slightly larger over-runner is driven further down. The partially assembled cask is now placed over a steam bell, and as the steam permeates the oak it becomes more pliable. The cask is now inverted in a mechanical clamp that pulls the staves into a barrel shape and the rest of the hoops are driven into place. Scottish casks were fitted with extra pitch hoops to provide further strength for the air-pressure system of dispense. Once assembled, the cooper uses a semi-circled crow plane specially designed to cut the groove around the ends of the cask, so that the heads can be fitted. Before the heads are fitted, the interior is smoothed with a roundshave so that no rough edges remain that can harbour bacteria.

The heads are made from boards that are dowelled together and shaped and chamfered so that they will fit tightly into the groove. The heads are always inserted with the joints running opposite each other, and cooper's rushes, or flags, are inserted into the groove and when wet they swell up, ensuring a good seal. After the cask is assembled, the tap hole and the bung hole are bored and brass bushes are screwed in. The bung hole bush usually has the brewer's name stamped on it for ease of identification. The stave ends are trimmed and angled, and the exterior might also be given a smoothing with a drawshave. Finally, the ends of the cask are painted, covering about half an inch over the heads, and this is necessary to prevent the ends of the cask from drying out.

Coopering was big and expensive business, and not surprisingly brewers in Edinburgh, Alloa, Aberdeen and Glasgow were the major employers. To cut down on the number of coopers and consequently wages, brewers increasingly made use of casks made in a steam cooperage, where each cask is made by a machine based upon geometrical principles. The machine can shape and chamfer a stave for any size of cask, shape and trim the heads, and automatically steam and raise the staves ready to be hydraulically pulled into a barrel shape. The grooves are cut by a chiming machine, and the finished product has been claimed to be superior to a hand-crafted cask. Due to austerity during the Second World War and the shortage of suitable oak, consideration was given to making casks from plywood that the Germans had successfully produced prior to the outbreak of hostilities.[32]

Casks are coopered in a variety of sizes, with quaint names that derive from the Old Dutch and the lowlands influence on British brewing. The term hogshead comes from 'Okshooft', a cask of 54 gallons. A kilderkin (or kyldekyn), 18 gallons, and firkin (Vierdekijn), 9 gallons, mean a half barrel and a quarter barrel of 36 gallons, respectively, and the term 'spile' also comes from the Old Dutch meaning a peg. The cooper takes great care to ensure that a cask does not hold less than the reputed volume. However, due to the fact that timber is liable to expand when wet and shrink when dry, it is impossible to guarantee that a cask will hold an exact measurement. To avoid problems with the Customs and Excise, coopers were allowed the following liberty when making new casks:

Hogsheads: 54¾–55¾ gallons
Barrels: 36¾–36½ gallons
Kilderkins: 18½–19 gallons
Firkins: 9⅜–9¾ gallons
Pin: 4½–5 gallons

By the latter quarter of the Victorian era, brewing processes and techniques changed to meet demand for India beers and light sparkling pale ales of moderate gravity. After 1880, we now see the use of flaked maize and sugar to dilute the protein levels in the grist, so that the brew did not require the same length of maturation time to achieve sparkling clarity. Such materials also diluted the nitrogen (protein) levels in the grist that helped secure microbial stability. All of this was also coupled to a drop in original gravity and elevated fermentation heats not too dissimilar from English practices, and fermentation times were reduced from twenty-one days to seven days. The elevated fermentation heats created substantial top crops of yeast that required skimming rather than being roused back into the brew as previously. Skimming was facilitated by drawing a skimming board across the surface of the brew, pushing the yeast head towards a copper or cast-iron parachute that dropped it into a collection vessel below. The yeast now entered a yeast press that compressed it into a paste for re-pitching, and the collected wort was returned to the brew.

In 1806, the first recorded evidence of scientific knowledge was brought to bear on the process of brewing when a report by those three eminent doctors, Hope, Coventry and Thompson, to the Scotch Board of Excise, was ordered to be printed by the House of Commons.[8] The introduction of breweries run by qualified chemists became widespread, although the setting up of laboratories was slow and many brewers had to be dragged into the new scientific age.

By the 1880s, the alcoholimeter was in use by major breweries and it was constructed on an empirical scale that indicated the alcohol by volume at 60°F (15.5°C). It was also used to determine the original gravities of a brew, testing rival brews for gravity, and to check that returned beer was not diluted or mixed with other beer qualities. The polarimeter was also used to determine the rotatory power of dextrin and maltose, plus other sugars, and this check helped the brewer determine the strike heat. Lovibond's tintometer was used to establish the colour of malt and beer to achieve consistency in the end product.

In April 1884, Louis Pasteur visited Wm. Younger's Abby and Holyrood breweries, and after the tour he praised the cleanliness of the vessels. After examining yeast with a microscope he pronounced it 'pure'. Around this time Mr J. Jacobsen of the Carlsberg Breweries in Copenhagen studied at Wm. Younger's brewery and went on to become a noted biologist. Wm. Thompson, who rose to the position of Head Brewer at Whitbread's Brewery in London, also studied at Wm. Younger's during the chairmanship of Harry J. Younger.

However, despite the best efforts of the brewers and chemists, it was inevitable that some beer would go off, or acidic, in the publican's cellar. In the case of returned beer, it was usual for it to be blended in, in various proportions, with stout where the sub-acid flavour was acceptable.

In 1889, Wm. Younger's employed the eminent brewing chemist John S. Ford, who is remembered for his invention of a model brewery, the Baby Ford, which could produce experimental brews from as little as 4lb of grist rather than a full brew of forty quarters. After brewing and sampling the trial brew, the Customs and Excise legislation required that the beer is destroyed. The other major brewers, such as McEwan's and Jeffrey's of Edinburgh, Tennent's of Glasgow, and Ballingall's of Dundee, also employed chemists to try and eradicate bacterial infections that could quickly destroy a brew and by judicial examination of brewing ingredients achieve consistency.

Apart from brewing manuals, conical flasks, pipettes, thermometers and saccharometers, the laboratory contained the all-important microscope that allowed samples of yeast, wort and beer to be closely examined for microbial contamination. The health of the yeast was also very important, and the microscope removed the guesswork and experience of judging the vitality of the yeast during fermentation. The chemist now had the means to identify healthy yeast cells, mutant cells, dead cells and bacteria, and take corrective action by washing the yeast in a mildly acidic solution that would knock out the bacteria but leave the yeast in a viable state.

Malt could also be checked out in the laboratory for its germination capacity. To do this the chemist conducted a mini malting procedure, and 100 to 200 corns were laid out between two layers of flannel and kept wet for twenty-four hours. Next, the water is drained and the corns kept at 50°F for forty to fifty hours. At this point at least 99 per cent of the corns should be sprouting. Anything less than this and the batch is rejected.

After malting, the grain underwent the 'sinker test', which was applied to test for dead or under-modified corns and worked on the theory that modified malt has a specific gravity somewhat less than that of water. Therefore, if a handful of properly modified corn is placed in water, they will float lengthwise, and poorly modified or dead corn will sink. Hard-ended corns will sink but will stand upright near the bottom of the vessel due to a small pocket of air that remained trapped in the end of the kernel. Good malt should not have more than 2–3 per cent of sinking corns, and the brewer can now calculate the quantities required for a brew· The sinker test remained in use until the 1950s.

The other major change that took place in the nineteenth century was in social attitudes, and brewers started to house their workers in accommodation and introduced better working conditions. Some examples are at the Clockserie Brewery, Perth, in 1837, when the brewer, David Mitchell, was provided with a cottage in Isla Road and the maltster, Thomas Clark, lived next door. In 1881, Ballingall's of Dundee built a house with garden for the capital brewer, Mr Stuart, and a tenement to house the head brewer and heads of other departments; the tenement still stands today. At the Edinburgh and Leith Brewery, the head brewer resided in the old mansion house that belonged to Sir Archibald Wardlaw (1793–1874) 17th Baronet of Pitreavie. Also, at this time the Bo'ness Brewery provided a house for the chief clerk. In Perth, the Craigie Brewery provided servants' quarters and cottages for married servants, and in Glasgow Tennent's provided housing for their labourers. At

Fowler's Brewery, Prestonpans, a house was built for the head brewer plus twenty-four cottages for brewery workers, and in Alloa, Jas. Calder built a house for the head brewer and cottages for his workers. By the twentieth century, this practice was common throughout the brewing industry in Scotland.

Brewery workers were also allowed a free allowance of two pints of beer daily that no doubt supplemented their meagre diet. However, this practice did not escape the clutches of the taxman, and by the 1950s the brewers were legally bound to tax the workers 3*d* per pint, which amounted to 2/9*d* (17½p) per five-and-a-half-day week. The more benevolent brewers repaid the workers in their wages.

The Victorian brewer was paternalistic, and the better-off was usually a philanthropist and became involved in public life and politics. Cynics will argue that they were simply watching their back! However, they did reap huge profits that afforded them the luxury of living in villas and mansion houses far removed from the often cramped and squalid dwellings of their workers. Some brewers, such as Morison's of Edinburgh, not only invested their profits in property but acquired a Highland estate, and it was not uncommon for them to close the brewery down for a couple of weeks during the shooting season and use the brewery staff as grouse beaters![39]

The period from 1880 until 1901 saw the building of some of Scotland's finest public houses of great character and charm, of which, sadly, few survive today. The archetypal Victorian pub, which was a throwback to the infamous Gin Palace, was a major step forward in the improvement of public houses, and what they were replacing was the dingy and squalid dens in closes, pends and back streets. Many of the new hostelries had elaborate frontages with polished granite pediments and pillars and stained-glass leaded windows. Also popular were large acid-etched windows with neo-classical designs that let in the maximum amount of light, and at the same time gave the toper the privacy he demanded and also prevented the public, particularly children, from viewing the drinkers and thus becoming corrupted!

The interior décor was artistic and luxurious, with high vaulted ceilings with brass gasaliers and lined with Lincrusta papers, or perhaps ornamental coffered panels with the cornice finished with a dentil course. The back fitments, or gantries, might command the whole bar and were built of foreign hardwoods, typically mahogany, and were elaborately carved, turned and finished off with finials. The bar counter was also made of hard-wearing French polished hardwood to support banks of hand pumps, which predated the tall founts that eventually became the norm from the 1870s until the 1990s.

A cork puller was required to open bottled beers and was to remain a feature in many pubs long after corked beers were discontinued. The spirits might be stored in ornate acid-etched glass decanters or in a small cask placed on the gantry. On the front of the bar there might be a brass handrail, and below that conveniently placed 'scratch plates' so that the topper could strike a match and light up his pipe or cigar. On the floor surrounding the bar there might be a brass foot rail and immediately below that a terrazzo sawdust trough or spittoon.

This was the height of the Victorian era, and was the golden age of shop design in general and pub design in particular; architects, decorative painters, signwriters, carpenters, glass stainers and embossers, were all working with a flourishing decorative tradition.[35]

When beer was delivered to the pub it was initially placed on the stillage and allowed to rest, to let the mad condition settle down. Thereafter, the publican would punch through the tut on the shive and insert a soft spile or peg that was cut from lorit (Limewood) that was porous and allowed the excess CO_2 to vent. With experience, the publican would judge the best time to insert a non-porous hard peg, made from oak, to seal the cask and retain sufficient CO_2 so that the beer would be served in a fresh and lively state.

The pub was a man's domain and this was reflected by the fact that most usually only had one toilet, which in some cases might also be outside. The inside toilet might be a grand affair, with massive china urinals designed concave to provide much privacy. They were regularly flushed out, with the waste water coming from the water engines that provided the air-pressure propelling the beer from the cellar to the bar. A privy was also usually provided, and to prevent any mischief one usually had to get the key from the barman.

Apart from the basic rectilinear bar, others might be in the shape of a horseshoe or an island, either octagonal or oval. The latter was the concept of Brunel, and was designed for railway stations to accommodate an inrush of thirsty travellers rather than have them queued out onto the platform. The

The Cromdale Bar, Dundee.

island bar usually had a central stock platform that acted as a support for spirit casks, which were also practical as well as ornamental. In some cases, the centre of the island bar housed a small manager's office, with small sliding screens through which he could keep an eye on the topers, and through which the barmen would pass the money and so have no access to the till! The bar counter might also be sub-divided with ornate 'snob' screens that allowed private conversation or perhaps a shady deal. The walls might be covered in heavily embossed papers or decorated in Art Nouveau style (1890–1910).

Attractive bevel-edged, acid-cut mirrors advertising brewer's ales and stouts, or Shilling Ales, were placed around the walls, and these reflected the soft gas light brightening up the interior. It has also been claimed that the mirrors were strategically placed so that the publican could keep an eye out for any mischief or inappropriate behaviour. A rip-roaring open fire in the familiar cast-iron and tiled fireplace provided the warmth that was so often lacking in the customer's home. It is no wonder, then, with such a display of opulence amidst the squalor of the times, that such establishments were dubbed the 'People's Palaces'.

Public houses were so named as they were open to the public, which meant that, in theory, anybody was entitled to enter, except that the publican could refuse entry to anyone without giving a reason. For the better class of establishment, they were patronised, although not exclusively, by affluent businessmen, the professional class, the managerial class, artisans and the suburban dandy, the philandering masher. The masher, which is a west coast term, belonged to the lower middle class and was impecunious but full of affections. He generally wore boots with pointed toes, excruciatingly tight trousers, a very short coat, a stupendously high collar and a bowler hat with a brim 'like a pig's tail', and considered barmaids to be his natural prey.[35]

Of course, all of this gives the impression that all Victorian pubs were luxurious, but this was far from the case and many popular pubs in rural and less socially desirable areas and county towns were very basic with drab interiors and sawdust-covered floors. The gantry might be made of softwoods, which was camouflaged with a coat of dark stain to create the warmth of mahogany and a lick of varnish in lieu of French polish, and in some burghs such grim conditions were encouraged to motivate temperance. In 1901, for example, the Dundee Wine, Spirit & Beer Trade Protection Association made the following comments in their response to the Magistrates' Report on the Administration of Licensed Premises in Liverpool: they pointed out that the Liverpool idea of having well-furnished and comfortable rooms for the accommodation of their customers was a successful one, and that the Dundee principle of abolishing everything which tended to comfort in a public house, and of making licensed premises as bare and unattractive as possible, has been followed in the city.

Despite such drawbacks, the publican kept a clean and orderly house and ruled his domain with a rod of iron. He was skilled in the management of cask-conditioned ales and stouts and kept a good pint. Nineteenth-century barmen were expected to work a sixty-five-hour week for what might be described as minimum wages.

Many of the dingy back street pubs were disreputable dens, full of whores and comic singers, and no respectful woman would dare to enter and those that did so were, rightly or wrongly, considered to be of ill repute. Some pubs had a snug bar, which was usually in the public bar area by the main entrance, so that women could discretely enter. It was sort of halfway between the public bar and the lounge, and was considered to be suitable for women accompanied by their men. Swearing was frowned upon and culprits were penalised by a token to the money box.

Of course, excessive drinking and drunkenness was widespread, and one idea that evolved in Sweden early in the nineteenth century was called the Gothenburg system, or Trust Public Houses. The following résumé is taken from an article that appeared in the *Dundee Courier* on 12 May 1899. In 1855, the Swedish government legislated against the distillation of spirits at home and the authorities in Gothenburg decided to award the retail spirit licenses to a single company run as a trust. The aim of the trust was to control public houses and off licenses in such a way that would not encourage excessive consumption of spirits. Shareholders were restricted to 5 per cent profits, and the remainder was to benefit the local community.

The principles of the Gothenburg system quickly caught on and eventually spread to Scotland, and were mainly implemented in the mining communities of the Lothians and Fife. Understandably, with so little profit, the managers of Gothenburg Houses were described as 'disinterested publicans'!

As the country started to recover economically after the Second World War, local authorities started to build huge housing estates and relocate families from the city centre where the housing, which was often owned by private landlords, was in many instances run-down and virtually uninhabitable. This paved the way for slum clearances, and although this was highly desirable, we lost too many old and beautiful pubs to the wrecker's ball.

During the twentieth century, and long before karaoke, it was usual on Friday and Saturday nights for entertainment to be provided in the lounge bar by a local music group and a 'weel-kent' regular acted as compere and invited people up to sing. Up until the 1970s, some jolly good sing-songs were to be had.

The lounge bar was considered to be upmarket, and this was reflected in an increase in the price of drinks. At weekends the lounge was usually restricted to women and couples only, to keep the troublesome philanderer at bay. The law stated that last orders were at 10 p.m., plus ten minutes drinking-up time, and this was rigorously enforced by the police.

The last quarter of the twentieth century brought in many sensible changes to the liquor laws, and the Licensing (Scotland) Act of 1976 gave local authorities the right to set their own opening hours. In October 1977, public houses in Scotland were allowed for the first time to sell excisable liquor on Sundays, since Sunday closing was made compulsory in 1853.

PROHIBITION

'Vote for good old Neddy, he'll not let you down.'
Election's cry of Edwin Scrimgeour
during the 1922 election

There is an interesting tale that after Charles II was crowned at Scone in 1651, Governor Lumsden of Dundee gave him refuge, and this raised the ire of Cromwell's man in Scotland, General Monk, who arrived with an army seeking revenge. The town was put under siege for two weeks until General Monk's spies informed him that the inhabitants were in the habit of enjoying a draught of strong ale for breakfast at 4½*d* per pint, which left them in a soporific state. He used this information to good effect and stormed the town, quickly overrunning the inebriated inhabitants without a fight and slaughtering about one fifth of the population. However, as the majority of the residents were poor, they could only afford cheap small beer and, consequently, it would take gallons to make them intoxicated, and the major risk to the town would be the diuretic consequences!

Due to the repugnance of the drunkenness and social degeneracy that prevailed during the nineteenth century, it saw the emergence of moderation societies, which were largely led by women, in Glasgow in 1829, followed by the Scottish Temperance League in 1844. Other movements followed such as The Good Templars, The Rechabites, the Band of Good

Hope and the Blue-Ribbon Army. As the temperance movement gathered pace it was having an influence on local and national politics, and in Dundee in particular the movement became very strong, with organisations such as the Dundee Temperance Society, the Gospel Temperance Vigilant Union, that became very political and at Perth in 1848, and the Total Abstenence Society.

The Dundee poet and tragedian, William McGonagall, couldn't resist having a dig at the demon drink when he penned the following in his enduring style.

Oh, thou demon Drink, thou great destroyer,
Thou curse of society, and its greatest annoyer,
What hast thou done to society, let me think.
I answer thou hast causted the most of ills, thou demon Drink.

Thou causeth the mother to neglect her child,
Also the father to act as if he were wild,
So that he neglects his loving wife and family dear.
By spending his earnings foolishly on whisky, rum and beer

And after spending his earnings foolishly he beats his wife,
The man that promised to protect her during life,
And so the man would if there was no drink in society,
For seldom a man beats his wife in a state of sobriety.

Unfortunately, McGonagall's poetry was enough to send people to drink!

In 1870, Hugh Ballingall of the Pleasance Brewery in Dundee was elected to the Town Council and he quickly became a target for the prohibitionists. In 1871, the *Dundee Advertiser* reported a verbal attack on Ballingall's probity at a public meeting on 4 April by the Rev. McNish in the Kinnaird Hall, by claiming that he was 'a man who was doing all he could to ruin the town, to add to taxation and to ruin the souls and bodies not only of themselves, but of all connected with them'. Not surprisingly, Ballingall was offended by such acerbic comments that labelled him as a person of bad character, habits and pursuits, and raised an action in Dundee Sheriff Court claiming £150 damages for slander.

Initially the Rev. McNish apologised, and tried to fob off Ballingall with two guineas that was to be donated to charity! However, finally the Reverend capitulated and offered the following apology:

> I hereby withdraw the said statements so far as they might be construed as applying to Mr Hugh Ballingall, brewer, Dundee. Personally, I regret that they should have been so expressed as to admit of any such construction, which could not have been my intention. I do not know Mr Ballingall personally and so far from having heard anything prejudicial to his private character, I believe him to be a gentleman deservedly esteemed by his fellow-townsmen.

No story about prohibition in Scotland would be complete with mentioning Edwin 'Neddy' Scrimgeour (1866–1947), who was the son of a local philanthropist and Bible-thumping Christian. He had a typical Victorian Christian upbringing and joined the Good Templars as a schoolboy. In his twenties he became a local politician in Dundee, and in 1901 he formed the

THE

PROHIBITIONIST

ADVOCATING

Prohibition of the LIQUOR TRAFFIC

No. 163. Vol. XIII. MARCH, 1915. ONE HALF-PENNY.

"RIGHTEOUSNESS IN ACTION."

Scottish Prohibitionist Party with Bob Stewart, who became secretary and organiser. In 1906 he published and edited *The Scottish Prohibitionist*, a weekly newspaper dedicated to combating the evils of drink. It was this religious, prohibitionist and socialist political activity that made Neddy popular with the electorate, although his first attempt to get into parliament met with failure. It was Neddy's religious passion that caused too much friction with Bob Stewart, and he resigned from the party in 1910.

In 1907, the Boroughloch Brewery, Edinburgh, closed and legend has it that the brewer, young Andrew Melville, fell hopelessly in love with a well-to-do American lady who was unfortunately fervently anti-drink. Regrettably, she would only agree to the marriage if Andrew gave up all connections with brewing and, presumably, he became teetotal.

Despite the resignation of Bob Stewart, Neddy believed that it was God's will that he should try again, and despite two further rejections in 1910 he remained undaunted.

Such was the furore that in 1913, prior to the First World War, the government introduced the Local Veto Option Polls that allowed residents to delicence public houses and in effect go dry. Neddy had nothing but contempt for the Temperance (Scotland) Act that was going through parliament, which gave residents the option to vote to stay wet or go dry. The Dundee Wine, Spirit and Beer Trade Protection Association raised a petition against the Act, and when the Bill was going through its second reading in parliament, social reformers were ask to invoke the Divine Blessing upon the deliberations of parliament! The Bill was passed and in the polling that followed and Wick, Lerwick, Kilsyth and Kirkintilloch voted to become 'dry'.

The election of 1918 was yet another failure, but he did secure twenty-seven percent of the vote and so he was encouraged to try again. By 1922 the country was still impoverished after the First World War, and the country fit for heroes failed to materialise. Neddy, who was now a Prohibitionist and Independent Labour candidate, swept the boards and unseated the sitting MP, Winston Churchill, and became Scotland's first and last prohibitionist MP.

After his maiden speech, Neddy went to work on his Private Member's Bill, The Liquor Traffic Bill, which tried to impose a penalty of five years' imprisonment should alcohol be sold for other than medical, industrial or scientific purposes. Needless to say, this Bill was heavily defeated. However, the election of 1923 saw Neddy returned to parliament with 40 percent of the vote, with further successes in 1924 and 1929. Again, he tried to introduce his Liquor Traffic Prohibition Bill, and again it was defeated. Two years later,1931, saw another general election, and quite unexpectedly there was a collapse in the Labour vote and Neddy was ousted. This ended Neddy's long political and prohibitionist career, which was also the beginning of the end for the Temperance movement as a whole, and it was defunct by 1935.

It is against this prohibitionist background that brewers became fearful that their livelihood might be threatened, and they started to appease the prohibitionists with non-alcoholic beers.[34] One of the earliest brewers to brew non-alcoholic beers was the Clydesdale Brewery of Glasgow, in 1908, which also changed the company's name to an anagram of Burton, 'Tonbur'! In 1910, Robert Deuchar bought out Simson & McPherson of Edinburgh, and in 1916 he brewed a non-alcoholic 'Sparkling Spring Light Ale'. In 1918, the firm of J.W. Carmichael, Edinburgh, produced 'wholesome and nutritious' non-excisable Lactic Stout.[12]

In Dundee, John Robb & Sons brewed a non-intoxicating 'Bitter Beer' using the finest English hops. Barrie's Aerated Waters Co. Dundee brewed non-intoxicating stout, and J&J Miller of Stirling produced Hop Ale. George Younger of Alloa initially leased Robert Wallace's Bass Crest Brewery in Alloa, and used it to brew non-alcoholic beer called 'Temperance (TS) Stout', which sold under the 'Pony' brand and remained popular from 1920 till 1943. J. & R. Tennent also ventured into the low-alcohol beers during the 1920s and 1930s with 'Malto', which was said to be a 'stimulating liquid food and valuable restorative for those physically and mentally exhausted'.

SCOTTISH INNOVATIONS AND TECHNOLOGY

'The Scots have always been an energetic and enterprising people and have contributed significantly to the technological development of the British brewing industry. After all, the Industrial Revolution actually started at Glasgow on the river Clyde.'

JA.

Hop Training

From the time Reynolde Scot wrote *A Perfite Platform of a Hoppe Garden* in 1574, hops were trained and tied to poles made of yew, ash and chestnut. The poles were 10–16ft (3–5m) long and were very expensive, with two to three poles per plant, which made a regular hop yard too costly for the ordinary farmer. Writing in the *Hop Industry*, Parker tells us that the Scotsman H. Home made one of the most original suggestions in the *Gentleman Farmer* in 1776, when he came within an ace of hitting on the idea of the wirework system of training hops. Home had been carrying out trials of training hops on an espalier system with a view to growing hops in Scotland. The espalier method, or lattice-like wirework, was hitherto used in the successful growing of fruit trees, and would alleviate the need for numerous poles. His work became the basis for future wirework systems of training hops.

THE EVOLUTION OF THE BURTON UNION SYSTEM

In the early farmhouse system, which was a primitive method in which the same tub was employed as mash tun and fermentation vessel, the beer eventually being cleared in the same cask from which it was stored and served. Initially, the beer was run, or ladled, from the copper into large casks, usually puncheons (72 Imperial gallons/327 litres) – a process called 'tunning'. The casks were referred to as 'loose pieces' and were placed on long wooden troughs called 'stillions', which collected the barm as it oozed out of the bung hole and ran down the outside of the cask. The casks were topped up every three hours or so, with great care being taken that the returned wort was as free of yeast as possible.

With the rise of the common brewers, the practices varied in that smaller trade sized casks for delivery to public houses were often used, and the method was also referred to as the 'carriage system'. Guinness used this system until 1834, and in The *Penguin Guide to Draught Beer*, 1978, Michael Dunn tells us that Bateman's of Wainfleet used this method until 1953! Clearly this system was satisfactory and the only reason for its discontinuation would have been the high cost of maintenance and labour and the demand for larger and quicker volumes of beer in post-war Britain.

Following on from the loose pieces, we see the development of the Ponto system, which is another old system of fermentation that took place in vessels called 'roundlets', 'rounds' or 'Pontos'. They were not strictly casks, but rather vats of six barrels' (216 gallons/982 litres) capacity that were slightly conical, which enabled the hoops to be well driven, keeping the vessel secure. On the head of the vessel was a wooden chute that allowed the top yeast to ooze over and fall into a trough below. The rounds might be arranged in groups of four, with the lips turned inwards so that the yeast fell into a trough in the centre. Alternatively, and possibly a later arrangement, the rounds were lined up in two rows facing one another and the yeast flowed into a central trough.

All of the above methods were labour intensive and required continual topping up of the vessels, and this led to the development of a self-racking method that consisted of a tinned copper cone, which was sealed with a bung, and also had a small pipe attached at right angles. The loose pieces could be filled using the cone and then sealed, and the small pipe directed the escaping barm into an adjacent trough, which served two bordering puncheons. The barm collected in the trough was returned to the cask via the cone, and from this arrangement we see the development of the Union system in its embryonic stage.

However, in 1838 a Scotsman, Peter Walker, who was a brewer in Liverpool, patented an idea that took account of the drawbacks of 'loose pieces' and the Ponto system that allowed the beer to be continually recycled without manual labour. He arranged the casks in two rows and each cask was fitted with a swan neck in the bung hole, which directed the overflowing yeasty beer into a trough above. The yeast slowly sedimented and the clear beer above ran back into the cask by gravity. Brewers throughout the land, including Ireland and Scotland, eventually took up Walker's patent and the brewers of Burton upon Trent in particular enthusiastically adopted the Union system, which was well suited to their fast non-flocculating type of yeast. Eventually the system became known as the Burton Union System.[33]

The Union system consisted of casks of four-barrel capacity (144 gallons) that were permanently secured on a rack in 'union' below a yeast trough, or barm back. They were designed with a tap hole and a bung hole into which was

Unions at Youngers Abbey Brewery, Edinburgh.

secured a 'swan neck', which would carry the beer from the cask into the trough above. Each head of the cask was fitted with trunnions, one that was square to facilitate a handle to rotate the cask for cleaning. To the underside belly a drain cock was fitted with a moveable tube that could be adjusted to project just above the sedimented yeast, which allowed the clear beer to be drained off leaving the yeast behind.

The fermentation starts off in a square until the wort has attenuated by 25–75 per cent. It is then racked into a feeder back and then into the unions, with the exception of two casks, which are reserved as 'cold ale' casks. The yeast used in the unions is of the fast type and during fermentation the beer is forced out of the bung hole by the evolving CO_2 and deposited through the swan neck into the yeast trough. The yeast trough was held on a slight angle to allow the beer to flow to one end, which was perforated with a number of vertical small holes sealed with corks. The cooling attemperator is also fitted to the barm back and this helps sediment the yeast in the trough.

Depending on the depth of the barm in the back a cork is removed to allow the relatively clear beer to flow by gravity into a feeder back. From the feeder back, the beer is run through 'side rods', which run round the union setts and are connected by running 'T's to the tap hole of each cask. Thus, we see a continual recycling of the beer flowing over the bed of yeast, and this is part of the reason for the unique flavour of Burton ales.

When there are obvious signs that the fermentation is slowing down, the corks are replaced in the barm back and the beer is run into the 'cold ale' casks, which keeps losses to a minimum. After the fermentation is finished the beer is run off via the drain cock on the underside of the cask into a trough that is connected to a racking back, or square. Yeast for repitching is collected from the middle layer in the barm back.

Apart from the huge costs involved, the Union system produced a sound beer with good flavour, and the main drawback was that the casks had to be cleaned in situ, which meant that if a large number of unions had to be cleaned at the same time, the heat given off by large volumes of hot water could raise the temperature of the fermenting room to an unacceptable level. Despite the drawbacks, the Burton Union system became very popular and Younger's of Edinburgh experimented with it, but their slow flocculating top fermenting yeast was not suited to the recycling system and the unions were discontinued.

Mashing Machine

In 1853 the engineer and brewer James Steel (1821–91) invented the external mashing machine (pre-masher) that consisted of a horizontal cylinder of iron or copper, with a revolving shaft to which is fitted an Archimedean screw and arms fitted at right angles. The grist and hot liquor are fed in at one end and forced

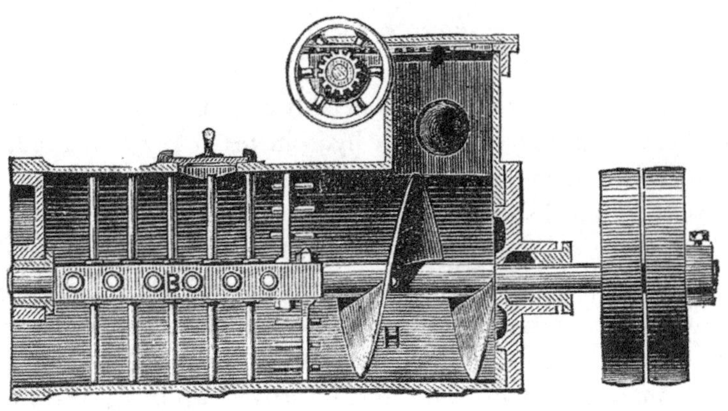

Steels external masher.

along the tube by the Archimedean screw, and intimately mixed by the side arms before falling into the mash tun.

This device saved on time and the laborious mixing of the mash with a hand-held rudder or oar. At the time Steele invented the pre-masher, he was brewing at Tureen Street, Calton, Glasgow, and in the same year he acquired the Greenhead Brewery from the Struthers family. In 1858 he acquired the Craigend Brewery in Edinburgh, and in 1865 formed a partnership with George Coulson of Croft-an-Righ Brewery, Edinburgh, to form Steel and Coulson & Co. Ltd. Unfortunately, the partnership failed due to Steel's acerbic behaviour. Steel is, however, the author of *A Selection of the Practical Points of Malting and Brewing and Strictures Thereon, for the use of Brewery Proprietors*, 1878. In 1936 the head brewer at Guinness's Park Royal Brewery, London, William S. Gossett, fitted a Steel's masher and it remained in use until closure in 1994.

Willison's of Alloa also produced an external mashing machine that delivered the liquor in a thin sheet and was also fitted with paddles to intimately mix the liquor and grist.

BREWER'S SACCHAROMETER

The saccharometer evolved from early experiments by Robert Boyle, who produced a simple hydrometer in 1675. In 1762, Benjamin Martin produced a hydrometer calibrated in specific gravity for the distillation industry.

However, despite suggestions that his instrument could be adopted for calculating the strength of beer, ale, wine and wort, Martin remained unconvinced and consequently gave up his experiments. James Baverstock then took up Martin's hydrometer idea in 1768 and improved upon it, and he became the first brewer to use one regularly to calculate the gravity of wort.

In the meantime, John Richardson had also been busy inventing a saccharometer that had a stem scale in brewer's pounds per barrel, which referred to the weight of a barrel of wort over the weight of a barrel of water. A gallon of water weighs 10 pounds and a barrel, which is a cask of 36 gallons, so that a barrel of water weighs 360lb. In Roberts's day a brewer could expect to extract 90 brewer's pounds of extract from one-quarter of malt weighing 336lb and, in this case, the saccharometer would record a total weight of 360lb plus 90lb = 426lb.

Therefore, to find out the yield from a quarter of malt the weight of water of 360lb is deducted from the reading on the saccharometer. For example, should the reading be 459, the yield would be 459 – 360 = 99 brewer's pounds per quarter.

To find the specific gravity (SG) we divide the reading of 459 by 360, which will give us the specific gravity in 36 gallons. For example: 459/360 = 1.275. For practical purposes brewers do away with the one thousand and so the reading to work on is 275 in 36 gallons. To find the SG of one pound of wort in one gallon would be 275 x 36 gallons = 9900, which equals an SG of one gallon of 9900/336lb = SG of 29.4 per lb/gal.

To convert degrees of specific gravity into brewer's pounds, subtract 1000 and multiply by 0.36.

Richardson's saccharometer led to significant changes in malting and brewing and he published his findings in his *Statistical Estimates* in 1784. Baverstock became outraged at Richardson's claim that he had invented the saccharometer, and in 1785 he published his *Hydrometrical Observations and Experiments in the Brewery*, to prove that he had been using a hydrometer in the brewery for the previous sixteen years.

Over time a variety of saccharometers appeared on the market based on Richardson's principles. However, such saccharometers were somewhat imperfect, which led Perthshire-born Dr Thomas Thomson (1773–1852) to invent a saccharometer and he enlisted Alexander Allan, an instrument maker in Edinburgh, to make the device for him and he named it after him. The Allan saccharometer was calculated on the difference in weight of a cubic foot of wort over that of a cubic foot of water at 60°F (15°C), but in this case the difference was measured in degrees of gravity. In time the saccharometer became gauged to the weight of 100 gallons of distilled water that weighed 1,000lb and this was converted into 1,000 degrees. As all other gravities were 'specifically' related to 1,000 degrees, their readings were termed 'specific gravity'. Whilst Dr Thomson's calculations were not one hundred percent correct, they were accurate enough for practical purposes and were in unofficial use by the Scotch Excise from 1805, and brewers referred to the gravity of their worts in 'degrees Allan'. Dr Thomson's instrument was officially accepted by the Scottish Excise by an Act of Parliament in 1815. On 5 August 1837, James Young, the head brewer at Truman, Hanbury and Buxton, London, wrote: 'I have been accustomed to the daily use of the Allan's Saccharometer for the last ten years and consider it an indispensable guide in the manufacture of beer and ale.'

It was also another Scots scientist, William Twaddell (1792–1839), who designed a hydrometer (°Tw) for measuring the specific gravity of liquids denser than water.

The Sparger

The familiar rotating sparging device, which sprinkles the mash with gentle raindrops of hot liquor to wash out the sugars from the goods, takes its name from the Laten '*Spargere*' meaning to sprinkle, and in Auld Scotch to 'spairge'. The sparger was in regular use in Scottish brewers from the early 1830s, long before its adoption by English brewers, many of whom considered it a loss of time. One of the earliest English brewers to adopt the rotating sparger was Messrs. Barclay & Perkins of the Anchor Brewery, Southwark, London, in the 1840s.

Just who invented the sparger is not known, but the early type was made by an Edinburgh coppersmith in Leith. The apparatus was supported above the mash tun on a central spigot and the hot liquor was initially discharged into a central copper pan, which was fitted with baffle plates against which the liquor impinged causing the apparatus to rotate

An early sparger.

on the spigot. As the sparger rotated, the hot liquor was thrown out into the sparge arms by centrifugal force, and as it leaked out through the perforations the jet-reaction setup also assisted the device to spin. Later, Willison's of Alloa advanced the technology with their 'ball and socket' sparger. By the 1880s we see the use of telescopic spargers that could be adjusted above the mash to improve the efficiency of the sparging.

STEAM POWER

In 1765, the Scottish engineer James Watt (1736–1819) improved on the Newcomen steam engine that had been in use since 1698 by adding a condensing chamber that made more efficient use of steam. In 1775, he formed a partnership with the Birmingham industrialist Matthew Boulton. In 1782, he invented the double-acting engine in which steam pressure acted alternately on each side of a piston. Boulton & Watt built up a fine business supplying steam engines to industry that became the mainstay of the Industrial Revolution.

The first brewery in Britain to employ a steam engine was the Red Lion Brewery, St Katherine's, London, in 1784. The first Scottish brewer to install a steam engine appears to be John Struthers, of the Gallowgate Brewery, Glasgow in 1797. When John Jeffrey built the Roseburn Brewery, Murrayfield,

Edinburgh, 1880, he installed a steam engine that amongst other tasks drove the steam cooperage and the hop press. Also in 1880, when Hugh Ballingall built the modern Park Brewery in Dundee, it too had steam power throughout, including steam-heated coppers.

COOLING

In 1837, Roberts mentions the use of a copper spiral pipe placed in a large tank of cold well water, through which the hot wort passes on its way to the fermentation vessel and is cooled to a pitching heat of 55°F. This method would also aerate the wort.

Later developments saw the introduction of horizontal refrigerators and two designs, invented by Morton and Smith respectively, became popular and could cool 2,520 gallons of wort per hour. In Scotland the coolers were principally manufactured by Stewardson & Hodgson of Edinburgh. The coolers consisted of a zigzag of flattened copper pipes through which cold well liquor at about 45–50°F (7–10°C) was passed throughout the length of the cooler. In another design, the cooler is divided by a number of narrow partitions, each section having the copper cooling pipes running through them. The cooler is set at a slight angle so that the hot wort enters at the highest end and slowly fills up the first compartment before overflowing into the next. This procedure continues until the wort reaches the lower end of the cooler and is discharged into the wort receiver. Wrights Brewery of Perth installed an open horizontal cooler in 1955.

In Bernard's Old Edinburgh Brewery at Slateford Road, he invented a cooler that consisted of a cast-iron box, 90'x4', with 150 copper tubes running the length of the case extending to 13,000ft. The hot wort was fed in at one end and the cold water at the other and could cool sixty barrels to 55°F in one hour. This must be one of the earliest forms of counter-flow cooling.

The large surface area of the coolers, which could be up to 10,000 sq ft, allowed the wort to lose its heat to the atmosphere and cool quickly, but it also increased the risked of infection by the thermophilic bacteria L. *delbruckii,* which can survive up to 50°C. It has been recorded that up to 140,000 organisms per hour fell onto the surface of wort in an open cooler.[28] A brew that had become infected was termed to have become 'foxed' as the pong given off by the bacteria was similar to the smell of a fox!

Another development was the vertical refrigerator invented by Baudelot in the 1870s. The vertical 'trickle' cooler entailed a series of round or oval-shaped copper tubes lying horizontally between two uprights. The cold water is run though the pipework, entering at the bottom and escaping at the top. The hot wort, which might initially be run from an open cooler, is fed into a trough at the top. The trough is perforated to allow the wort to sparge evenly over the length of the cooler and trickle down over the cooling pipes. The pipework might also be designed in a single or double 'S' to increase the surface area for cooling.

The trickle cooler at the Half Moon Brewery, Bruges.

The small vertical cooler installed at Traquair House Brewery, Innerleithen, Peeblesshire, was donated to the brewery by Sandy Hunter of the Belhaven Brewery, Dunbar, in 1984. The cooler was originally used in a dairy to cool pasteurised milk and was acquired by Sandy Hunter and used at Belhaven for a number of years.

However, at this time scientists were looking at ways of producing mechanical refrigerators, and in the early 1870s the German firm Vaass & Littmann produced the absorption refrigerator, but it was prone to malfunction and did not operate satisfactorily in warm weather. About the same time, Dr Carl Von Linde had been working on improving a French refrigerator, and by the end of the decade Linde refrigerators were installed in the Carlsberg Brewery in Denmark where they worked very efficiently and reliably. Artificial cooling was now desirable in all continental lager breweries, but it didn't take the British too long to appreciate their usefulness in the production of good ale.

Ice-making refrigerators came into regular use during the 1880s and ice-cold water or brine was passed through the coolers to effect a rapid lowering of the wort temperature. The ice-cold water was usually stored in a refrigerated room in lead-lined tanks, and could also be used to chill the fermentation squares, settling squares and casks in the cellars.

THE SHILLING TERMINOLOGY

Money, pre-1707
1*d* = 1/12th Sterling
2*d* = 1 Bodle/Turner. 1/6th Sterling
2 Bodles = 1 Plack, 1/3rd Sterling
3 Bodles = 1 Bawbee, ½ Sterling
2 Bawbees = 1/- Sterling
13/4*d* = 1/1½ Sterling
20/- = £1, 1/8*d* Sterling
The merk (mark) = 13½*d*

Money post-1707
Pound = 240*d* = 20 shillings = a Sovereign, aka a 'quid'
Half Sovereign = 10/- = 'ten bob'
Crown = 5 shillings = 5/-, or 'five-bob'
Half-Crown = two and six = 2/6*d*
Shilling = 1/- = 12*d* = aka a 'bob'
Sixpence = 6*d* = aka a 'tanner'
Groat = A silver coin worth fourpence (4*d*)
Threepence (Thruppence) = 3*d*
Penny = 1*d*
Halfpenny = ha'penny = ½*d* = a 'Bawbee', a bawbee was also a name for a dowry
Farthing = quarter-penny = ¼*d*

Historically, brewers the length and breadth of Britain sold their beer by the shilling. Also, both Scottish and English brewers produced penny ales, and so the use of our currency to describe a brew is not exclusive to Scotland and the question remains: what is it that makes the Scottish shilling terminology unique from other parts of the United Kingdom?

No one sat down and devised the shilling system, and this intriguing terminology simply evolved as a means of identifying a type of beer within the trade. Prior to 1880, Scottish brewers priced their beers according to the cost of raw materials. Prior to 1862, this included a hop tax plus the tax on malt and sugar and a percentage profit. The malt/sugar tax was based on the yield from 84lb of malt or 56lb of sugar, which produced a gravity of 1.057 in the standard barrel of 36 Imperial gallons. The gravity of 1.057 was the average gravity at this time but was later reduced to 1.055. The bulk barrel was a 36-gallon cask of beer of any gravity. The duty was due immediately after the Exciseman recorded the malt in the couch frame. For many brewers this was a huge outlay, and consequently it was only the wealthy brewers who could afford to pay the increased duty on high-gravity beers and then store them for up to a year to mature.

The wholesale price of the beers produced until 1880 ranged from 28/- ale, 36/- ale, 40/- ale, 42/- ale, 48/- ale, 50/- ale, 54/- ale, 56/- ale, 60/- ale, 70/- ale, 80/- ale, 90/- ale, 100/- ale, 120/- ale, 140/- ale, 160/- and 200/- ale. In these examples we can see that the price ascended in a linear manner according to the progressively increasing gravity of the beer. In cases where the number of shillings fitted neatly into the pound (20/-), the brewer might also categorise the beer accordingly; thus, 60/- ale = £3 ale, 80/- ale = £4 ale, 100/- ale = £5 ale, 120/- ale = £6 ale, 140/- ale = £7 ale, 160/- ale = £8 ale and a £200/- = £10 ale, and we can see an example of this in the inventory of Robert Stein's Edinburgh brewery cellars in 1819 that recorded 104½ barrels of £5 ale and 82 barrels of £6 ale.

It must not be overlooked, however, that the original gravities of all beers were probably never fixed due to seasonal variations in the harvest, which resulted in various degrees of extract recovery from the mash tun. It is unlikely that the brewer would have dropped his price for a batch of beer that did not have the same gravity as the previous brew. The quality and price of the hops, too, varied due to harvest conditions, their age and transport costs by sea. The number of hops employed also varied with the season and weather conditions to promote the antiseptics and preservation of the brew. However, it would also be wrong to suggest that all brewers produced the full range, although most would have brewed the lower gravity beers for what would have been a lucrative market catering for the humble masses.

The old pricing system remained in force from 1830 to 1880, when the government accepted the saccharometer as an accurate instrument for measuring the gravity of wort. Consequently, the Chancellor of the Exchequer, William Gladstone, repealed the tax on malt and sugar and replaced it with duty on original gravity and volume. The initial duty was levied at 6/3*d* per standard barrel, and the duty on other gravities was levied pro rata.

However, the old malt/sugar tax was still retained and was applied in cases where it gave a higher tax rate than the duty based on original gravity. At this time brewers throughout the UK continued to invoice their beer by the shilling, but it was during this period that the Scottish shilling terminology slowly came into being. The phraseology was primarily trade lingo and simply evolved as the brewer, who was largely a wholesaler, and the publican, who in general ran a free house, negotiated over the price of the beer.

As Edinburgh had some forty breweries in the 1880s, the terminology would have most likely developed there and slowly migrated to other brewing centres. Therefore, we can see that as the numerous free trade brewery representatives bartered with the publican, it became necessary to avoid the confusion of everybody attempting to describe the beer they were offering by referring to it by the new price or its gravity.

However, the exact time that the jargon came into common usage is not known, but there may have been a time when the wholesale cost of a barrel remained fairly static and gravities were either at, or reasonably close to, the wholesale price for a range of beers costing a number of shillings.

Also, in Wm. Younger's brewing notebooks the grist for malt and hops and the gravity of the brew varies throughout the year, and so there was never a fixed recipe formulation for any type of ale. In consequence, each brew would cost a penny or so above or below the typical wholesale price, but the brewer no doubt would keep the retail price the same. It is also well known that a brewer going through a bad batch might lower the gravity of his beer to save on the cost of malt and hops.

For example, should the wholesale price of a light beer in shillings cost 59/11½*d*, or 60/2*d*, would it not be simpler when negotiating to round off the price and simply refer to the beer as 60/- ale? Such an approach would be of little consequence as the wholesale price was only a starting point in the negotiations that took place to determine the invoice price. Consequently, as haggling was taking place over the invoice price of a barrel of beer, it was obviously easier to continue to refer to a light brew as 60/- ale, regardless of its gravity or wholesale price. This approach was also used for all the beers in the shilling range. Also, the volume of beer that the publican could sell largely determined the invoice price. A small back-street tavern with a low turnover would not receive the same discount as a large city centre pub shifting lots of beer, and it is known that the latter might secure a discount of up to 50 per cent per barrel.

With the passage of time the terminology stuck, and eventually became accepted under the Finance Act of 1914. However, with the ever-increasing costs of raw materials, duty and slowly diminished gravities, particularly during the First World War, the terminology became meaningless, although the jargon continued as a trade means of identifying a type of beer until the 1940s. Consequently, 60/- ale in the 1880s remained 60/- ale in the 1940s, although the gravity was significantly attenuated and the price greatly inflated!

The range of beers that existed after the 1880s was a variety of weak table beers such as 'Tippeny' (twopenny ale) or 'Pundy' and fourpenny ales, which were produced from the second mash of strong ales, retailing at 24/-, 28/- and 36/- per barrel. Mild ales retailed at 40/-, 42/- and 70/- for strong mild. Pale ales retailed at 48/-, 54/-, 56/-, 60/- and extra hopped pale ale at 80/- all priced by the barrel. In the early twentieth century, Wm. Younger's 40/- and 50/- ales were popular in Aberdeenshire and other northern counties at harvest time, and sold at 3*d* per pint.

The system was further complicated in that beer sold to licensed grocers, bottling firms and publicans for bottling was usually delivered in hogsheads, a cask volume that is 1.5 times a barrel, or 36 gallons x 1.5 = 54 gallons. The beer at this stage now underwent a change in designation and a hogshead of light beer did not become 54 gallons of 60/- ale, but rather 60/- x 1½ equalled 90/- ale! By the same token a 70/- ale became 105/-ale (Strong Mild) and an 80/- ale became 120/- ale.

Taking a 48/- ale as an example, it would be recorded in the brewer's log as 72/- ale and not as a 48/- ale. Part of the reason for this is that by this time the trend was moving towards the use of adjuncts such as white maize and Martinaeus and Demerara sugar, to dilute the high protein content of local and imported barley that was very important for the clarity and stability of bottled beer, which was by now becoming very popular. Mash heats, too, were lowered somewhat to reduce the final gravities, which meant that bottled beer had a slightly lighter character. This meant that although the brew was essentially 48/- ale, the modifications to the recipe for bottled beer meant that the two brews demanded a different title to avoid confusion. Categorising beers in this way meant that when a 72/- ale was being brewed all brewery staff, from the head brewer to the cellar staff, were under no doubt that the brew was for bottling and not a 48/- ale for casking. The cellar staff would also ensure that the brew was racked into hogsheads before delivery to bottlers, and equally importantly the bottler, and in particular the publican, would know that the cask was for bottling and would not be tapped for draught.

That the trend was steadily moving towards bright beer is evidenced in the *Brewer's Almanac*, 1895:

> It is, however, essentially within the last ten years that these lighter ales, both of pale ale and mild character, having come especially to the front. The public in this period has come to insist more and more strongly upon extreme freshness of palate with a degree of brilliance that our fathers never dreamt of.

When beer was casked in a hogshead it might also be named by the guinea, a coin that was equal to twenty-one shillings (21/-), although it was no longer legal currency as in 1816 the Chancellor of the Exchequer, Nicholas Vansittart, introduced the Imperial Coinage Act that discontinued the guinea and replaced it with the sovereign, which was equal to twenty shillings (20/-). The guinea did, however, remain as a pricing currency well into the twentieth century. Consequently, a hogshead of 63/- ale divided 21/- became Three Guinea Ale, 84/- ale became Four Guinea Ale, and 105/- ale, strong mild, became Five Guinea Ale. Very strong bottled ales such as 168/- ale, 210/- ale, 252/- ale and 315/- ale retailed at 8, 10, 12 and 15 guineas respectively. It is also interesting to read that veterinary surgeons often gave Twelve Guinea Ale to aid stricken animals! In the twentieth century, strong ales eventually became known as Dumps, Nips or 'Wee Heavies', although such terms are rarely used today.

However, it can be confusing when we see advertisements on old bottle labels, pub mirrors and windows for 90/- ale and 120/- ale. This is often mistaken by the ill-informed as advertisements for strong ales, and whilst this might have been relevant before the 1880s, it is not the case under the shilling terminology and what is being advertised is bottled 60/- ale and extra-hopped export 80/- ale respectively. In 1891, publican Alexander Stewart of Stewart's Vaults, 133 City Road, Glasgow, bought 125 hogsheads of McEwan's 90/- Edinburgh Ale for bottling, which was a complete March brewing!

The practice of identifying bottled beer by the number of shillings continued up until the 1960s, and J&J Morison's produced a 90/- Ale 'Bottled by the Brewers'. McKay's of Edinburgh still produced bottled 90/- pale ale and Bernard's of Edinburgh brewed a light bottled ale called 90/- India Pale Ale, a title that is ridiculous for a light ale. Also, Scottish and Newcastle breweries brewed a bottled 90/- Ale called 'Sparkling Ale'. However, the original Sparkling Ale was an 80/- ale first brewed by Wm Younger's of Edinburgh in 1852 for a customer in New York. Of course, it is confusing to read 90/- India Pale Ale, or 90/- Strong Ale, as this does contradict the foregoing information, although strong 90/- ale was available prior to 1880.

However, having discussed this enigma with brewing historian Charles McMaster, our conclusions were that this was simply an advertising ploy. We also discussed this with Sandy Hunter (1920–2007), former owner and chairman of the Belhaven Brewery, Dunbar, and he thought it more of accountant's dodge.[31] Sandy Hunter's opinion has to carry considerable weight as his father, Ellis Hunter (1877–1964), would have been brewing since the turn of the century and the shilling terminology would have been well known amongst the late Victorian and early Edwardian brewers and staff, and the history of the terminology would have been passed onto his son.

It has to be remembered that at this time there was no legal (or moral!) obligation for brewers to declare the strength of their beers or put the minimum contents of the bottle on the label. A label might only state that the bottle was simply a container for beer! The lack of a trade's description acts also meant that brewers were free to call their beers by any misleading name or description they liked. However, it should not be forgotten that the shilling terminology was largely restricted to the trade and the public would not have understood it. Before the introduction of pump clips, the topper simply asked for a pint of draught by name and price, such as draught mild at 4*d* or pale ale at 7*d*, or bottled beer by the price per bottle.

By the time bottled beers became increasingly popular after the First World War, the new generation of brewers either did not know the shilling terminology or were not too concerned about it as it was largely irrelevant. Consequently, misconceptions crept in and abuses on labels became prevalent. During the 1930s bottled beer became very popular and was advertised according to price, thus we saw 4*d*, 5*d*, 6*d* and 7*d* ales.

I feel much of the present confusion surrounding the shilling terminology arises from the manner in which the Wm Younger recipes are tabled in the second edition of *Old British Beers and How to Brew Them*, which gives the impression that the system was linear. This was not the case after 1880, and it should be noted that virtually all the beers in the publication date from 1871 to 1872, long before the inception of the shilling terminology. The shilling system only lasted from 1880 until the 1940s and, consequently, it is misleading today for a brewer to call strong ale 90/- ale under the shilling terminology.

Finally, the vexed question often arises: why did English brewers not identify their beers by the 'shilling' or guinea? In the first instance, some did! For example, in 1865, Brakspears New Street Brewery, Henley on Thames, brewed a 50/- ale and a 140/- ale.[27] Also, prior to the First World War, Benskin & Co, Watford, brewed a No. 2 Guinea Ale, and the Shropshire Brewery also brewed XX Guinea Ale. Hardy & Hansom produced Guinea Gold Ale and Guinea Ale.

However, English brewers historically designated their beers by type but retailed them by the shilling. The Scots, though, traditionally brewed and sold their ales by the shilling, and in a city like Edinburgh, for example, which had numerous breweries all vying for trade in a thriving free market, competition was fierce. Consequently, as previously discussed, the jargon simply evolved from the bartering process into a type of beer.

The shilling terminology has been somewhat controversial and some historians have quite rightly questioned it. What is often quoted is the fact that porter and stout were also named in shillings, and references are made to the cellars of Robert Stein in 1819 where we see the following: 115/-, 90/, 80/-, 40/- and 30/- porters sold by the barrel. However, the date is 1819, which is sixty-one years before the inception of the shilling terminology. Others refer to early twentieth century examples whereby McLay's brewed a 54/- pale ale and a 54/- stout, and Usher's produced 60/- pale ale and 60/- mild ale.

In all these examples, they must have had a similar gravity and price, and in any case, they were all 'mild ales' that were sent out to the trade shortly after being brewed, and such beers by the twentieth century became known as 'running ales' as opposed to stock ales that required maturation.

Guinea ales, too, were typically naturally conditioned beers and were also sold as bottled and draught. The Edinburgh & Lieth Brewery produced a Seven Guinea Ale, and in 1886, Ballingall's of Dundee were advertising their Eight Guinea Ale, which was in first-rate condition for sending out in wood or bottle. One should be cautious about such statements as it is most unlikely that the strong draught was served by tall fount or handpump, and more typically it went to the publican for bottling or the cellar in the 'big house', or the pin sat on the bar counter or gantry and was served in half pints. Strong sales were often used in beer mixtures.

MILITARY ASSOCIATIONS

'Over 50% of Great Britain's beer exports and practically the whole of the bulk beer consumed by our troops abroad are exported from Scotland.'

Robert Bruce, 1939

An early reference to the military and brewers in Scotland is in 1550, when Scottish soldiers and French mercenaries stationed at Dunbar Castle were supplied with beer from Belhaven. Also, when Cromwell's forces took a sojourn in Edinburgh after the Battle of Dunbar (1650), he billeted his troops in the maltings of the Leith Brewery and the sleeping quarters were in the barley stores in the attic. Wounded and sick troops were hospitalised in the cooperage that was still called the infirmary in the 1800s.[8]

The British forces have always provided brewers with an outlet for their products and to secure the contract of supplying a ship, garrison or units in the field was an important and lucrative business. Good beer was a great morale booster in times of conflict, and during the Crimean War (1853–56) Scottish brewers stiffened the spine of the Scottish regiments with Scotch Ale before the triumphant battles of Alma, 20 September 1854; Balaclava, 25 October 1854; and Inkermann on 5 November 1854.

After the Crimean War, trade with the military increased, particularly for Wm. Younger's, and they had regular customers in the 91st Argyshire Highlanders; the Duke of Edinburgh's regiment; the Kings Dragoon Guards; the Royal Engineers; the 7th Queen's Own Hussars; and the 79th Queen's Own Cameron Highlander's. Comments such as 'well-liked', 'first-rate', 'very-good' and 'greatest satisfaction' summed up the soldiers' liking for the ales of Edinburgh.[34]

Local outlets were also important, and as infantry travelled long distances on foot a draught of good ale was always welcome at the end of the day. In 1857, during the four-month voyage to India to quell the mutiny that had erupted in May, the Black Watch were supplied with a daily pint of porter. Also, on one occasion in 1860 when four companies of the Royal Highlanders (the Black Watch) rested at Edinburgh, Wm. Younger entertained them with food and beer at the Abbey Brewery.

In 1874, Wm. Younger was supplying beer to the Argyllshire Highlanders, the Duke of Edinburgh's Regiment and the Queen's Own Cameron Highlanders. In 1881, during Queen Victoria's infamous 'Wet Review' of the Scottish Regiments, which was held in Queen's Park below Salisbury Crags (Arthur's Seat) in 1881, the Edinburgh brewers generously supplied the troops with ale and Wm. Younger billeted the London Scottish Volunteer Rifles regiment in the Abbey Brewery. When the Black Watch were stationed at Shoreditch prior to embarkation for the Peninsular Wars, they were issued with a daily pint of porter prior to training.

Of course, many other Scottish brewers were supplying the home garrisons and also exporting beer to the colonies, and so the volume of sales must have been huge. Wm. McEwan in particular secured major contracts with the military at home and overseas, and such lucrative contracts allowed him to build up a successful business that eventually rivalled Wm. Younger.

The importance of the quality of the beer for the Indian Army contracts meant that the importers laid down strict schedules for the brewing and transportation of draught ale to the colony. James Steel of 'masher' fame tells us that in the first instance the casks had to be coopered from the best Memel and Bosnian oak, and had to be free of worm holes and steam-seasoned and pickled before use. The ale had to be all-malt with a gravity of 1.060 and 20lb per quarter of the finest English and foreign hops. Frosty weather was considered best for brewing and keeping beers as the fermentation remained cool, and so brewing did not start until after 1 November and the brew was racked into casks not later than twenty-one days after the date of brewing.[58]

A problem facing brewers exporting ale in the best Memel oak was the non-return of casks, which incurred a huge loss to the brewery. Consequently, many brewers simply exported their beers in inferior casks to avoid such losses, and this might be part of the reason why so much beer arrived at its destination in poor condition.

When a beer was brewed for bottling it might be brewed from October until May and matured for at least a year, so that it should undergo a summer's heat and a spontaneous secondary fermentation in the autumn, which would attenuate and stabilise the gravity prior to bottling. This meant that a beer brewed during October or May was fully ripe for bottling the following October or May, although in some cases the brew might be eighteen months old before it was fully ripe and mellow. During maturation in oak the beer flattened sufficiently to allow bottling and corking prior to shipping, and this approach superseded the old method of allowing bottled beer to stand uncorked to flatten, which in theory prevented corks popping during the voyage, but left the beer prone to infection.

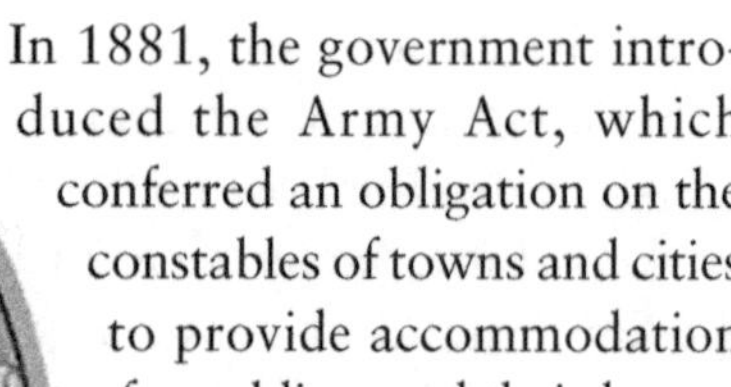

In 1881, the government introduced the Army Act, which conferred an obligation on the constables of towns and cities to provide accommodation for soldiers and their horses in victualing houses. The keeper of the house was obliged to provide food and accommodation for officers and men, and was to be reimbursed by fees authorised by parliament. Should a housekeeper feel aggrieved at having to put up too many soldiers, he could appeal to the Justices of the Court.[3]

In October 1892, a minute of the Dundee Wine, Spirit and Beer Trade Protection Association shows that members were raising questions about the allowance paid to public housekeepers for billeting soldiers. The following year the topic was raised again, and it was pointed out that soldiers going to and from Barry (by Carnoustie) were billeted in Dundee, and that no other group of traders had to tolerate this. In 1894, a publican brought up the fact that he only received 2/1*d* for billeting two soldiers instead of the usual 3/6![3]

By the early 1890s, Scottish brewers were the main suppliers of ale to troops in India, with the total overseas markets reaching over 167,000 barrels per annum. In keeping with the colonial times, Scottish brewers gave many of their export beers names indicating military or colonial connections, such as George Younger's 'Revolver Brand', or the 'Arab Brand', 'Khaki Ale' and 'Battleship Beer'.

Apart from charitable military causes, many of the brewers and their sons gave military service to the Crown. In general, the Victorian and Edwardian gentleman brewers followed the typical social protocol of the times by having the one son to enter brewing, another son to join the military, and if there were a spare, he might become a minister of religion. Daughters were encouraged to marry the best sociably acceptable male, who was very often from a brewing family, and such nuptials were more often than not financial contracts.

Some examples of brewing families and military service are that in Dundee, Hugh Ballingall of the Park & Pleasance Breweries was an ensign of the 10th Forfar Rifle Volunteers, and his third son, Henry (Harry) Millar, was an officer in the military who fought with distinction during the Boar War, winning a DSO and ended his career as a lieutenant-colonel. Captain David Reginald Younger of Edinburgh fought with the Gordon Highlanders during the South African War and posthumously won the Victoria Cross. Prior to the outbreak of war in 1914, Lt-Col William J. Younger took command of the Royal Scots and won a D.S.O. John Wm. Younger served in the Royal Artillery. Overall, some eighty of the Younger's staff volunteered for service during the First World War, and in 1917, Ferguson, who was the board's youngest member, was killed in action.

The other causality of the First World War was the dire shortage of raw materials for brewing, as the government commandeered the barley and wheat stocks to feed the population. By 1917, things got so bad due to the German U-Boat blockade that the government put a stop to malting altogether. The vice-chairman at the time, J.C. Younger, joked: 'Output dropped to a minimum and we were all guided into the doubtful pleasure of "Munition Ale".'[34]

Also, during the First World War, Scottish troops did not appreciate English ales and they demanded ales from their homeland to bolster moral and alleviate the hardship of the trenches. As anyone who has gone on a First

World War battlefield tour in Belgium will know, the reason Scotch Ale is popular and is now brewed in that country is because the Scottish troops demanded their own style of beer and Scottish/Belgium brewers satisfied that demand. Consequently, today, we still come across Campbell's Scotch Ale, Younger's Scotch Ale, McEwan's Scotch Ale and Gordon's Scotch Ale in Belgium.

In 1921 the Navy, Army and Air Force Institution (NAAFI) was formed to oversee the supply of goods and victuals to the British armed forces. By the 1930s such was the demand from the armed services for Scottish beer that McEwan-Younger Ltd was formed to handle this lucrative trade. During the Second World War, the NAAFI supplied some 380 million bottles of beer for the troops, which was enough for a glass of beer for every adult person in the world, and Britain contributed about 23 per cent of the totals, with Canada, the USA, and Australia and South Africa supplying the rest.[36]

Throughout the Second World War, beer was sent to the troops fighting in North Africa, whilst combat units in Northern Europe and Italy were supplied from local breweries whenever possible. In 1944, Winston Churchill visited the troops in Italy, and he was so besieged by requests for beer that on returning home he instructed every brewery in Britain to allocate 20 per cent of all bottled beer for the troops.

During the Burma campaign, British troops were allocated an abysmal three pints a month, which was simply not enough and, also, getting this to the troops was very difficult in the jungles and razor-backed mountains of Burma. One idea, introduced by Lord Louis Mountbatten, was to keep supplies as close to the action as safely as possible, and this involved the ingenious idea of mobile breweries. This concept was basically a home brewery mounted on the back of 3/4-ton truck designed for pulling 25-pounder artillery pieces! As one can imagine, keeping a good pint in the blistering 95°F heat (35°C) was extremely difficult, and one clever idea used by the Cameron Highlanders, and presumably others, was to wrap bottles in a wet straw basket and hang it on the back of vehicles so that the draught chilled the beer by evaporation.

With the war in the Far East dragging on, the Admiralty conceived the idea of a floating club and brewery to provide rest and recuperation for the troops. The 13,000-ton ocean liner *Menestheus*, which was built in 1929 by W. B. Thomson & Co of the Caledon Shipyard in Dundee for the Blue Funnel Line, was adapted for minelaying at the outbreak of war in 1939, and in 1943 it was converted into Davy Jones Brewery!

The floating brewery was an ingenious concept in which distilled seawater was used in conjunction with malt extract and hop extract to produce palatable mild ale within nine days. The brewing copper, which had a capacity of almost 2,000 gallons, was steam-heated from the exhaust of the ship's boilers. Fermentation took place in six glass-lined vessels and up to 1,800 gallons

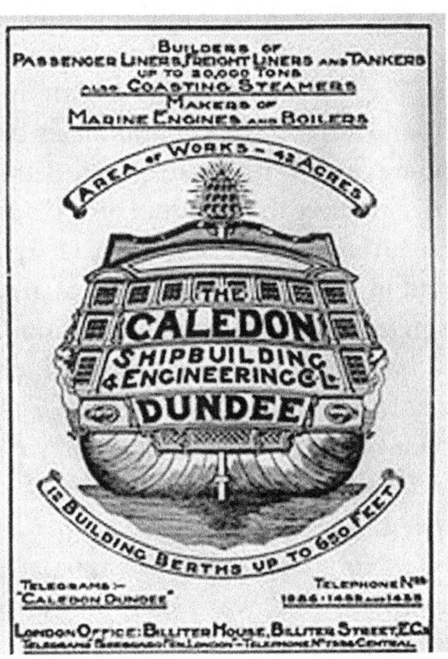

Dundee, the home of the Menestheus.

of mild ale, with a gravity of 1.037, could be brewed in one day. During one five-month trip the *Menestheus* served more than 40,000 men.[25] When the *Menestheus* was broken up after the war, the brewing equipment was bought by Calder's of Alloa.[39]

However, brewing at sea was not a new idea, as in 1778 R. Thorton introduced a patent for concentrated wort, for the purposes of making good and wholesome beers at sea and in distant climes and countries. The wort was reduced to a form similar to toffee, and when reconstituted and fermented it produced the genuine pure flavour of malt and hops. Throughout 1779–81, Thornton's extract was issued to the Royal Navy as an antiscorbutic to prevent scurvy.[15] During Captain Bligh's ill-fated voyage on the *Bounty* to Tahiti, sailors who showed early signs of scurvy were immediately doctored with essence of malt, and when the conditions inside the ship became wet and miserable the sailors were given a pint of sweet wort that was mashed daily. By 1798, the use of wort was discontinued when lemon juice (Vitamin C) was found to be more effective.

During the Second World War, on the east coast of Britain, German submarines, e-boats and aircraft were continuously on the lookout for Allied shipping, but Wm. Younger defied the Nazi threat and continued to ship beer to London. During one returning voyage in May 1941, the *Royal Fusilier* with a cargo of empty casks was sunk, and in June the *Royal Scot* was also lost. In February 1945, the SS *Egholm* left Leith and was sunk with a total loss of 17,730 barrels of Younger's ales, which consisted of 33 hogsheads, 215 barrels, 311 kilderkins, 264 firkins and 52 pins. In addition, the *Egholm* was also carrying 28 hogsheads and 50 kilderkins of McEwan's ales destined for military export. The following month the SS *Crightoun* was also sunk with a similar loss.[34] Notwithstanding the appalling loss of merchant seamen so close to the war's end, they also lost almost 36,000 barrels of beer, which was not only needed to boost the morale of the war-weary Londoners but much would also be sent to the victorious troops in Europe.

After victory in May 1945, Europe descended into the Cold War and the Navy, Army and Air Force Institution (NAAFI) supplied servicemen in the British Army of the Rhine (BAOR) in West Germany with Double Diamond, Herforder, Dortmunder, Amstel Bier and Pilseners. In 1955, Scottish Brewers Ltd secured the contract to become the main contractors to supply beer to the Army and Navy. Apart from British beer, the troops in Cyprus drank mostly Keo Lager, in Singapore and Malaysia it was Tiger Beer, and in Hong Kong it was San Miquel Lager.

COMMEMORATIVE ALES

Commemorative ales are brewed to celebrate a coronation or the birth of a royal heir, or a visit to a brewery by an important royal or foreign dignitary. Majority ales also celebrate the birth of a brewery's first-born inheritor and are matured until his coming of age, which used to be twenty-one years but in 1989 this changed to eighteen years. Such brews were brewed to a high gravity and matured in oak until the heir reached his majority. Brewer's might also produce a special birthday label to celebrate an important timespan in the brewery's history.

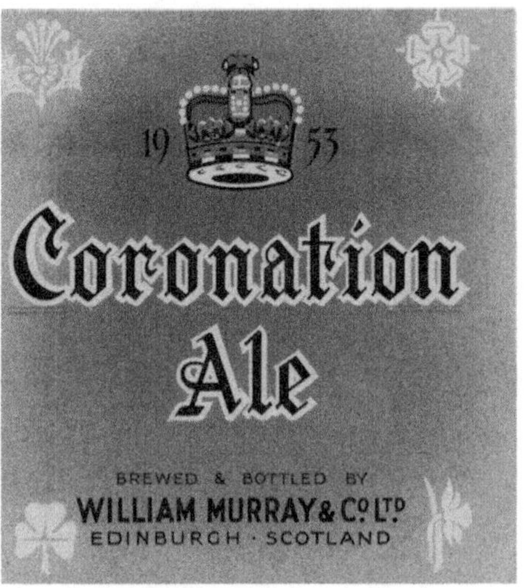

A Coronation Ale was brewed by virtually every Scottish brewer as a mark of respect to the new monarch, and was brewed for King Edward VII in 1902; King George V in 1911; King George VII in 1937; and Queen Elizabeth in 1952. The brewing of Wm. Younger's Coronation Ale in 1937 and Majority Ale in the same year would have been supervised by head brewer James Kerr Stevenson, affectionately known as 'Stevie' to all employees, who was head brewer from 1919 until 1945. Double Century Ale was first brewed to celebrate Younger's 200th birthday in 1949, under the supervision of head brewer William Ferguson.

BREWING LIQUOR

'All the beers are excellent. These are in such case remarkably pure and you need not have any concern as to their stability. I am extremely glad that you have succeeded so well with the new water, and that your beers are so satisfactory.'

Extract from report by analyst on samples of beer brewed from the above water at Robert Knox's Forth Brewery, Cambus, June 1892

Historically, brewers simply used whatever water was available, such as rivers, burns, and ponds or mill lades. River and burn water were considered best, as long as it was free from sullage. The fact that a specific type of liquor proved to be suitable for a particular style of beer has been recognised but not fully understood for centuries. It was only in the late nineteenth century, however, that the chemical composition of water was analysed, which clarified the effects it had on mashing reactions, hot and cold breaks, and how it accentuated or inhibited the flavours obtained from the malt and hops.

In the 1100s, the monks of Holyrood Abbey sunk a well 200ft deep that was still producing good liquor after 800 years, and the liquor was used to brew their famous export 'Monk' brand that was distributed through their London Depot. The Belhaven Brewery at Dunbar in East Lothian originally drew its liquor from a well sunk by Benedictine monks in the thirteenth century, and Wrights Brewery, Perth, was built on the ancient site of Blackfriars Monastery and they drew their liquor from an old artesian well. In 1543, when St Mungo, who was born in Culross ('Currous'), south Fife, founded his monastic community on the site of present-day Glasgow, the monks brewed with water from the Molendinar Burn. The ancient Blackford Brewery drew its soft water from the Danny Burn that is still used by the modern Tullibardine Distillery built on the same site. When the Clockserie Brewery at Bridgend in Perth was established in 1837, it used the water of the common Clockserie Burn. The Traquair House brewery, Innerleithen, still draws its liquor from a natural spring in the grounds of the estate that is piped some one and a half miles to the brewery, and likewise, Young and Company of Inverness drew their water over quarter of a mile from the River Ness. By digging a well, brewers gained access to the abundance of pure liquor in the water table, which meant that it was free from pollution and suitable for brewing. The depth of the well was not in itself important as long as it produced a constant supply.

In due course, brewers had the technology to bore artesian wells, which are usually bored to a depth of 328–985ft to penetrate a porous stratum consisting of sand, chalk, gravel and limestone. The term 'Artesian' is derived from the town of Artois in France, where exists the oldest known well in Europe at 343m (1,126ft) deep. One of the oldest wells in Edinburgh belonged to Bell's Brewery, Est. 1837, in the Pleasance, which was 500ft deep, and one of the deepest was at Campbell's Argyle Brewery, Chambers Street, sunk to 750ft. Some breweries might have two, or more, adjacent wells connected to collect water from different strata to extract hard and soft water. In 1880, when John Jeffrey gave up brewing at the Grassmarket and moved to the Murrayfield Brewery at Roseburn, such was the quality of the liquor that he retained the rights to all the water below the Grassmarket site and pumped it to the new brewery at Roseburn.

When J. & R. Tennent moved their brewery from the ancient site established in 1556 to the adjacent Wellpark site in 1885, they sunk a 1,000ft (304m) well to tap the remarkably pure soft water. Around 1892, Calder's of Alloa sunk a well with a bore of 906ft (276m), and in the same year George Younger of the Candleriggs Brewery in Alloa sunk a bore of 1,120ft that produced up to 6,000 gallons an hour. Wrights Brewery in Perth successfully drilled an Artesian well that was the town's only private water supply.

Much has been written about the hard waters of Edinburgh being similar to those of Burton upon Trent, but such information is misleading and this myth is still being peddled to this day! Most of the water drawn from the so-called 'charmed circle' was good brewing liquor simply because it was very pure in biological terms, with a constant temperature of about 10°C. Edinburgh lies in the centre of the heavily faulted north-dipping strata of Lower Carboniferous and upper Old Red Sandstone. The liquor drawn is characterised by the presence of sulphates linked to sodium and magnesium rather than calcium as at Burton, containing greater proportions of carbonate and increasing quantities of chloride. In its natural state the liquor is more akin to that of the carbonate liquor of Dortmund, which is well known for its malty golden lager, and so it was well suited for brewing the typical malt character of Scottish pale ale.[28]

However, none of the following waters could be described as perfect for brewing, and we can see in Lloyd Hynd's table for Old Red Sandstone that it contains sodium sulphate (Gloubers salt), which is unpleasant, although its sulphurous notes would no doubt be subdued somewhat in the old heavy bittersweet ales.

In all three examples, calcium carbonate dominates, and from the late nineteenth century onwards Edinburgh brewing chemists added lots of calcium sulphate to counter its ill effects on mash reactions, which resulted in poor mashing efficiency and consequential low extract recovery. Further additions of calcium sulphate were added to the copper where it would create a further decomposition of the carbonate to lower the pH of the wort to a value that would achieve good hot and cold breaks, and also secure microbial stability and a flavour-some bright beer of character. None the less, there would still be residual carbonates present and such hardness produced good hop-accented beer. To quote Lloyd Hynd, 'Edinburgh is well known for its pale ales.'

Chemical	Salt	Edinburgh Old Red Sandstone	Bell's Brewery, Pleasance, 1908	Morningside bore water
Sodium nitrate	NaNO3	41 mg/l		
Sodium chloride	NaCL	100 mg/l	104 mg/l	8 mg/l
Sodium sulphate	Na2SO4	128 mg/l		
Magnesium sulphate	MgSO4	180 mg/l	190 mg/l	24 mg/l
Calcium carbonate	CaCO3	350 mg/l	269 mg/l	135 mg/l
Magnesium carbonate	MgCO3		116 mg/l	79 mg/l
Magnesium chloride	MgCL2			24 mg/l

Do note that calcium sulphate ($CaSO_4$) is noticeably absent in the above liquors, and that the predominant salt is calcium carbonate ($CaCO_3$) or chalk. Also note that Morningside liquor is much softer than the Old Red Sandstone. In the case of Bell's Brewery, the chemist added 500–570mg/ltr of calcium sulphate for pale ales, which increased the hardness by 290–330mg/ltr to achieve good mash tun conversions. A further addition of 56g of $CaSO_4$ was added per barrel to achieve a further decomposition of the carbonates present during coppering, and to obtain a good hot break and achieve stability and brilliance.[46]

To demonstrate that the Edinburgh brewing liquors are not similar to those of Burton on Trent, the following tables are taken from an analysis of wells in the town centre by E. Brown and published in *The Geology and the Mineral Waters of Burton on Trent and Brewing Science & Practice* by Lloyd Hind, 1943.

In the following table we can see the waters of Burton upon Trent contain large amounts of calcium sulphate, with lesser amounts of magnesium sulphate, sodium chloride and calcium carbonates. Such gypseous waters are considered hard waters and permit the use of a high hop rate or hops with high resin content without fear of harsh flavours. Consequently, gypseous liquors are considered hop wasters, as the full brewing value is not extracted during coppering.

Chemical	Salts mg/l	E. Brown	H. Lloyd Hind
Calcium sulphate	CalSO42H2O	1109,6475	589,95
Potassium sulphate	K2SO4	22,6575	
Sodium sulphate	NaSO4	145,4925	
Calcium carbonate	CaCO3	108,585	235,125
Magnesium carbonate	MgCO3	303,6675	
Magnesium sulphate	MgSO4		299,25
Magnesium chloride	MgCL2		9,9975
Sodium chloride	NaCL	55,575	47,025
Sodium carbonate	NsCO3	28,0725	41,325

Today the Charmed Circle is no more, as the shale bed has shifted, and this coupled to the seepage of modern industrial effluence allowed the wells to become polluted and unsuitable for brewing. In 1873, Robert Wallace of the Bass Crest Brewery, Alloa, categorised three sources of well liquor that he found to be excellent for the main types of beer brewed.[46]

Overall, the natural Alloa waters are superior brewing liquors to those of Edinburgh.

Brewing liquor at the Bass Crest Brewery, Alloa:

Salt	Chemical	Pale ale	Mild ale	Stouts
CaSO4	Calcium sulphate	365 mg/l	288 mg/l	21 mg/l
CaCO3	Calcium carbonate	144 mg/l	151 mg/l	40 mg/l
MgSO4	Magnesium sulphate	644 mg/l		
MgCl2	Magnesium chloride		65 mg/l	9 mg/l
MgCO3	Magnesium carbonate		51 mg/l	5 mg/l
NaSO4	Sodium sulphate	18 mg/l		21 mg/l
NaCl	Sodium chloride	52 mg/l	4 mg/l	123 mg/l
NaCO3	Sodium carbonate			207 mg/l
KSO4	Potassium sulphate	36 mg/l		
KCI	Potassium chloride	4 mg/l		
K2CO3	Potassium carbonate			36 mg/l

On the mountainous west coast, the water was generally very soft, which made it ideal for Scotch ales, porter and stout, and eventually lager beer. After the City of Glasgow was supplied with the sparkling and pure soft water from Loch Katrine, brewers capped their wells and drew their liquor from the municipal supply. When India Pale Ales came into vogue, the soft liquor on the west coast was not ideal for its brewing, and consequently east coast brewers who had harder water found the Glasgow area a lucrative market for their IPA.[39]

YEAST

'Life is mostly froth and bubble!'

Adam Lindsay Gordon, 1833–70

CYTOLOGY

Of all the ingredients used in brewing, yeast must be the most complex and fascinating. It is a unicellular microscopic organism that only measures 3–7 microns in diameter and it is, therefore, invisible to the naked eye. It has its ancestry in the kingdom '*Protista*', which includes plants, animals and fungi. Fungi are 'eukaryotic', which means they have a true membrane-bound nucleus (unlike bacteria, which do not possess a true nucleus and are called 'prokaryotic'). Yeasts are eukaryotic, as are moulds such as penicillin, and the *Basidiomycetes* that include mushrooms, puffballs and shelf fungi; the latter is the familiar 'cork-like' growth that we see growing on the north side of trees.

Yeast, moulds and fungi do not contain the green pigment chlorophyll, and so are unable to photosynthesise sunlight as a source of energy. Therefore, unlike plants with roots, leaves and connective tissue, yeast leads an autonomous lifestyle and individual cells are to be found in abundance in the atmosphere, in the soil, water and on fruits.

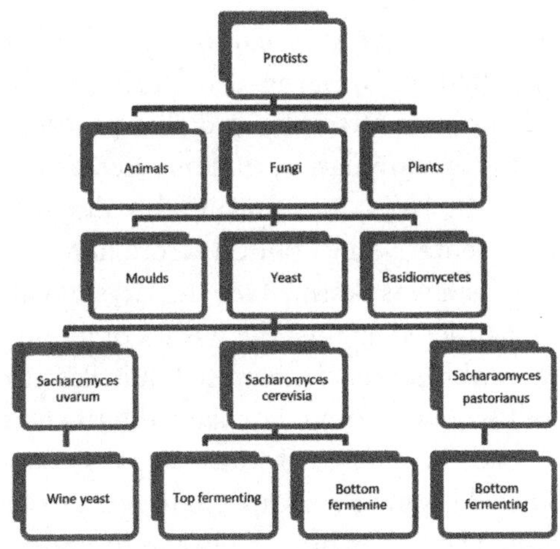

Yeast was examined for the first time in 1680 by the Dutchman Leeuwenhoek using a crude microscope, and he found that it consisted of spherical bodies, which he was unable to distinguish from starch cells. In 1818, Erxleben was of the opinion that yeast was of a vegetable nature that caused fermentation. During 1836–37, Schwann proved that fermentation was due to the presence of living organisms (yeast). In 1838, Meyen considered yeast to be a fungus and described it as *Saccharomycetes*, or sugar fungus. However, in 1845, Roberts wrote in *The Scottish Ale Brewer* that fermentation was still a mystery, and also wrote:

> For as much as has been written concerning fermentation and confidently as many have asserted their knowledge of its secret causes and effects, the mystery in which its principles are involved continues to present an impregnable barrier; and those who dogmatically profess to have compassed this subtle and complicated subject, only prove the extent of their ignorance and presumption.

In 1869, Wm. Younger was using yeast from Haldane's, Campbell's, Aitcheson's, Bernard's, Drybrough's, Ritchie's, Jeffrey's and Blair and Dick's, and this practice produced yeast with a diverse population that as often as not produced mixed results.[46] In 1874, and presumably due to stale yeast, Younger's representative in London wrote home complaining that the beer, which was destined for the Crystal Palace, was so bad that it was ordered against the wishes of his advisors.

It was not until the French chemist Louis Pasteur published *Etudes sur la Biere* in 1876 and explained fermentation as 'life without air', and the eminent Danish scientist Emil Christian Hansen produced his pure brewing culture free from wild yeast and bacteria in 1882, that brewers began to understood what yeast was and how best to maintain it in good condition and minimises the risk of infection and off flavours. Consequently, brewers could now reuse the same yeast, and as it was in continual use in the same plant it adapted to the environmental conditions in the brewery and slowly developed into a house strain.

Yeast, however, which was called 'store', and still is in Guinness breweries, is a fickle organism that is very prone to infection, and should it become contaminated with wild yeast and bacteria the results are unpleasant flavours in beer. To try to avoid disagreeable flavours, nineteenth-century brewers regularly acquired yeast from another brewery that was known to be sound. When brewers stopped production during the summer months it would be nigh on impossible to store yeast in casks or stone jars in the brewery, as it would quickly go rancid. In this case, fresh samples would be acquired from barm brewers who continually propagated yeast for the baking industry. Brewers also reciprocated by suppling the baking trade with yeast. Even as late as the 1960s, home brewers relied on baking yeast.

In the mid-nineteenth century, pitching rates depended on the quality of the yeast and, for example, a 100/- to 160/- ale, boosting gravities from 1.095 to 1.125, typically used three gallons of yeast slurry to twenty gallons of wort. However, if the yeast was thought to be in excellent condition this was reduced to avoid racing fermentations. Likewise, to control the cool fermentation profile, brewing was restricted to the colder months of the year from October to April, and in the case of stock beers and export beers preferable in frosty weather with an ambient of about 5.5°C (42°F).

Historically, and on average, the Scots pitched their yeast at around 50°F (10°C) and 'high Krausen' rarely exceeded 63°F (17°C). Such a cool fermentation meant that it might take up to twenty-one days to fully attenuate the brew, which contrasted with the typical English practice of fermenting at 65°–73°F (18–23°C) for about seven days. The cool fermentation also meant that yeast metabolism was slow and did not produce excessive amounts of fruity esters or harsh-tasting fusel alcohols and diacetyl, although nineteenth-century brewers did not understand this and they would simply detect differences in the flavour of the brew fermented at both extremes. For India beers, the pitching heat varied from 58–60°F depending on the quantity of yeast employed and the ambient temperature.[55]

In the early years, brewers did not appreciate the importance of aerating their wort before pitching the yeast, and a satisfactory degree of aeration simply took place naturally as the wort cooled in the open horizontal cooler. If a vertical 'trickle' cooler was used, the wort quite naturally absorbed a further small but sufficient amount of oxygen to satisfy the fermentation. Overall, the level of oxygenation would have been fairly low, which restricts yeast growth and the production of unwanted flavoursome esters. However, according to Southby in the late 1880s, the deficient aeration of wort in the Scotch system led to an unpleasant yeasty flavour often found in Scotch ales, which could only be cured by a change of yeast.

Due to the minimal levels of oxygen in wort and the cold fermentation, the result was limited yeast growth and flocculation, which meant that the top crop was fairly light and, consequently, skimming was rarely performed (unless it was necessary to check a too vigorous fermentation) and the top crops were regularly roused back into the wort to ensure a regular fermentation and attenuation. As the yeast was repeatedly used in strong brews, it meant that it developed a high tolerance to alcohol, and by the late 1850s Scotch Ale brewers increased the fermentation heats to quicken the attenuation so that stocks were adequate to meet the demand for Scotch Ale in England and compete with Burton Ale.

By now the classic approach to brewing was to employ two sets of fermenting tuns with one surmounting the other, and when the primary fermentation in the upper tun was ready for skimming it was dropped into the lower tun. This method was called the 'dropping system' and left the primary yeast in the upper tun and thoroughly roused and aerated the brew, and as soon as the new yeast head formed it was skimmed off. The skimming or flattening squares were much shallower than the fermenting squares, which facilitated a quicker separation of the yeast from the beer, which was now racked directly into the trade casks. In this case we are talking about 'running beer', which was beer for quick consumption, and such beers were second to none in flavour, condition and brilliance. After the First World War, the economic situation influenced Scottish brewing techniques and fermentation profiles to come in line broadly with English practice.

Yeast performance characteristics developed from various fermentation systems that evolved in certain districts, and Burton yeast is fast non-flocculating and ideally suited to the Union system that attenuates to the quarter gravity stage. Yorkshire yeast is weakly attenuating and ferments more slowly, and consequently requires regular rousing to sustain the fermentation that terminates at about one third of the gravity. London yeasts are similar to Scottish yeast, with intermediate properties.[28]

With the demise of the traditional brewing industry in Scotland during the 1960s and 1970s, virtually all of the original yeast strains have gone. As previously discussed, Traquair House brewery originally used Belhaven yeast, but as difficulties were experienced keeping successive brews free from infections in the ancient wooden brewery vessels, the yeast was eventually replaced with Nottingham dried yeast.

In 1979, Belhaven Brewers, Dunbar, lost all of their original yeast due to infection and had to acquire yeast from Drybrough's. Drybrough's yeast was harvested from their multi-vessel continuous fermenter and was ideally suited to batch top-fermentation. When Drybrough's closed in 1987, Belhaven acquired its yeast from McEwan's, and it has now developed into an individual house strain.

Taking advantage of the popularity and demand for cask ales in Scotland, the Broughton Brewery was established in 1979, and initially they used McEwan's yeast but subsequently brought in yeast from Vaux in Sunderland in 1985. The Vaux yeast has now been in continuous use since then and has developed into a separate strain (R388), which is freeze dried by a company specialising in yeast technology and is propagated as required at the brewery.

Lorimer and Clark's Caledonian Brewery, Edinburgh (1865), were taken over by Vaux of Sunderland in 1946 and they introduced their own strain of yeast. In the 1990s, Vaux yeast was changed for Ansell's yeast from Burton on Trent in order to brew beers under contract for Carlsberg-Tetley. Perhaps the only true historic Scottish yeast left is McEwan's, which was used at the Caledonian Brewery, Edinburgh, for McEwan's 80/- Ale and, presumably, used by the English brewers, Marston's, who now own the McEwan's portfolio. It has long become acclimatised to conical fermenters, but is also used by the York microbrewery where it has reverted to top-fermentation.

For Scotch Ales and India Pale Ales, the brewer requires a yeast that is alcohol tolerant, one that flocculates well and will ferment between 10–15°C and has fairly low attenuating properties. For the lighter gravity beers of the twentieth century, the criteria are not so important. Yeast that is regularly used in light gravity beers slowly loses its vitality and requires a fermentation in wort with a gravity of at least 1.055 to re-energise.

True brewing cultures are desirable for their purity and flavoursome fermentation by-products. Also, as the top-fermenting strains flocculate well and continue to separate from the wort, floating on top of the brew, the yeast head requires to be roused back into the brew to ensure a regular attenuation. This characteristic has the advantage that we can control the racking gravity, which is typically 3° above the final gravity. This is achieved by stopping rousing at a pre-determined gravity of about 6° above the final gravity and gently cooling the wort to 15°C that will further restrict yeast growth and encourage flocculation of the yeast, so that it rises to the surface and forms the 'closed head'. The closed head protects the beer from oxygenation and aerial infection. A further cold rest of 24–30 hours at 10°C will precipitate the yeast and nitrogenous debris to a point where that remaining in suspension will efficiently coprecipitate with isinglass finings.

As the sedimented yeast from the primary stage of fermentation is contaminated with nitrogenous debris, and the yeast forming the closed head is weak and oxygenated, the brewer selects yeast for repitching during 'high Krausen', the period of 52–72 hours after pitching, when the cells are most active and healthy.

The amount of pitching yeast is important. The problem with under pitching is that it leads to extensive yeast growth, which produces more aromatic beers as large amounts of unwanted esters are produced. Low pitching rates also lead to a long lag phase, which runs the risk of competing bacteria infecting the brew. High pitching rates can lead to the yeast undergoing autolysis, particularly if the temperature is allowed to rise above 23°C. If too much yeast is added, the cells multiply very slowly, as they struggle to compete for nourishment and this results in a lack of vigorous new cells necessary to rapidly metabolise the wort, and the quantity of yeast after fermentation is little more than that at pitching.

A sound fermentation should be well under way within 8–12 hours and should be regular with a steady attenuation and a good covering of surface yeast that should last, in the case of true top yeast, to the completion of the fermentation. With dried yeast, the head has usually sedimented by the end of the fermentation, which leaves an insignificant amount on the surface, and the brew should now be protected from aerial infection. In all cases the aroma of the brew should be clean, bready and yeasty.

In days of old, many fine types of ales had a subtle yeast nuance that contributed to the overall quality of palate. Some brewing systems such as the Yorkshire Square system and the Burton Union System acquired this quite naturally due to the continuing recycling of the beer over the sedimented yeast in the trough above. In Scotland, however, this delicate bite was acquired by regularly rolling the casks, which kept the yeast in suspension and thereby imparting its character into the beer, and such beers were sought after by the connoisseur.

To ensure that the beer drops bright in the publican's cellar, the use of finings is employed. The finings are primarily isinglass, which is the soluble colloidal material from the swim bladder of some varieties of fish, dispersed in an acid solution. The Russian sturgeon is considered the finest, but most species came from the Far East, with Long Saigon Leaf being a close second. Some other species are Penang Leaf, Penang and Bombay Purse, East India Pipe, Maracaybo, China Leaf, and from South America, Brazilian Lump.

To make the finings, the bladders are first dried and shredded and then steeped in a solution of tartaric and sulphuric acid. In olden times lactic and acetic were used in conjunction with sour beer, but this is now obsolete due to the risk of infection and lack of effectiveness in the low-gravity beers of the twentieth century.

Traditionally, the shredded bladders were placed in an unheaded hogshead or an earthenware vessel and covered with water. Next, 2lb of tartaric acid is stirred in, followed by 2 gallons of sulphuric acid, and the mixture is left to soften, a process called 'cutting', for up to six weeks. Regular stirring and the addition of water as required and the temperature is never allowed to rise above 55°F or the collagen will degenerate into gelatine, which is much less effective in clearing beer. After cutting, the mixture is forced through sieves with stiff brushes and broken down to 54 gallons, and finally sieved and diluted down to 6 barrels (216 gallons) with a consistency of Gloy Office paste or thick wallpaper paste. We now have isinglass that was added at about 2/3 pints per barrel to achieve rapid clarification in the cellar.

Just how fish bladders were discovered as a means of fining beer is a bit of a mystery, and how it worked gave rise to many theories. At the turn of the twentieth century the theory was that the isinglass rapidly sedimented at the pH of beer, and as it did so it formed a coagulum with yeast and protein debris and settled out rapidly. In 1927, the theory changed to one of electrostatic interactions between positively charged isinglass and negatively charged yeast that cancelled each other out, so that the neutral flocs that formed rapidly sedimented. Today we are still no further on, and the behaviour of isinglass remains cloudy. What is currently being investigated is initial electrostatic action coupled to hydrophobic interactions with soluble material that form flocs, which ensnare yeast and nitrogenous matter and drop out rapidly.

Isinglass finings are usually preceded by auxiliary finings that prepare the beer for a more efficient clarification. Previously it was thought that they acted in a similar way to isinglass, but it is now known that as they carry a negative charge and the beer also has a negative charge, they cannot electrostatically bond and will repel one another. It is now thought that they might react with positively charged soluble materials that would otherwise interfere with action of isinglass, or that they might produce complex reactions during the flocculation of isinglass.[1]

In what has been a rather conservative industry, brewers differed in their approach to the processes, including when best to add finings. In *Brewing, Science and Practice*, Lloyd Hind states the practice of priming, fining and shiving at racking for immediate dispatch was common with light gravity mild ales. But bitters, after a short period of storage, are finally primed, fined, topped up and re-shived for dispatch. In *Brewing, Theory and Practice*, Jeffery is quite adamant that no attempt should be made to fine down beers that show any degree of fermentation as such a practice is a waste of finings.

Scottish brewers did not use isinglass for Scotch Ale or high-gravity guinea brews that require long-term maturation, as the yeast and fine nitrogenous matter settle out quite naturally and, in any case, it was considered that finings robbed the beer of body, condition and character. After the finings were added in weaker brews, it was customary to roll the cask to bring the yeast and fine nitrogenous matter into solution to thoroughly combine with the isinglass. If dry hops were added, then they too assisted the fining action by providing attraction sites for yeast and protein debris.

With the introduction of low-gravity beers for quick consumption in the late twentieth century, the use of finings became more of a necessity. For best results, the finings are added to cool beer, which allows the finings to work more efficiently on a rising temperature as the beer warms up to cellar temperature. The reasons for this are as follows. When beer is cold, or better still, chilled, it maximises the amount of chill haze particles that will come out of solution, which increases the ease of entrapment when finings are added. When finings are added, the collagen ensnares the chill haze particles and as the brew warms up so are the collagen reactions speeded up, which further increases the entrapment reactions. Isinglass finings are most active as the temperature of the beer rises to 13–15°C.[1] The isinglass will continue react at higher temperatures, but this is not desirable as its structure becomes compromised, and in any case, nobody likes warm beer! Should finings be added to warm beer, the chill haze particles remain in solution and so do not become entrapped by the collagen. Consequently, when the beer is cooled or chilled before supping, it suffers from, at best, a degree of opalescence, or at worst chill haze.

SCOTCH ALE

'... having a paleness of colour and mildness of flavour, the taste of the hop never predominates. The low heat at which the tun is pitched confines the brewing to the colder months of the year. No summer brewing except for table beer and no strong ale is brewed or delivered.'

The Art of Brewing, David Booth, 1829

No one sat down and invented Scotch Ale, it simply evolved over a period of time from pre-thermometer mashing practices up until the introduction of hops in the early 1700s. The historical approach to mashing was to rouse as much malt as possible into the liquor in the mash tun, which resulted in a very stiff mash with the liquor grist ratio being as low as one to one. The mash heats, which were empirical and based on experience, were rather high by today's standards and were later judged to be typically 180°–190°F (82–87°C), and both practices resulted in a thick, sweet, dextrin-rich wort.

Groot was the ancient bittering material, but there is no historical evidence to tell us what the amounts were or what its mixture might have been. Judging by available accounts, the brew was heavy and sweet, a characteristic that we still see in Scotch Ale today.

After the introduction of hops, both hops and groot would have been used together for some time, including hops substitutes. The amount of hops used would have had the approximate bittering power of the groot that it had to replace, to ensure continuity of bitterness. Over time it became evident that hops were superior to groot for preserving and flavouring beer, and it was quite natural that they should become the principal material to use. By the early 1750s, brewers were adding 4lb of hops per quarter, but the quantity was never fixed as it depended on the quality of the beer and whether it was to be brewed during the winter or spring.

By the turn of the nineteenth century, the overall quality of Scottish beers had improved immensely and Scottish brewers increased their trade with the English market, and it was Robert Meiklejohn of the Bass Crest Brewery, Alloa, who was the first Scottish brewer to ship beer to London. In 1802, Wm. Younger of Edinburgh had established the Edinburgh Ale Vaults opposite Somerset House in the Strand, London.

The year 1821 saw an increase in the export market, but it was only the larger breweries with ready access to the sea that made a success of the export trade. George Younger of Alloa had one advantage in this respect, as he could export directly from the brewery's private jetty. Calder's Shore Brewery also had export cellars by the quay that could hold some 6,000 barrels ready for shipment, and was also famous for their Bee Brand in cask and bottle. The Edinburgh brewers McEwan's and Campbells, plus Dudgeon's of Dunbar, Tennent's of Glasgow and provincial brewers in Dundee and Brechen, Montrose and Aberdeen had established a thriving export trade. At this time it was said that the strong ale of Montrose was 'esteemed by good judges equal to Burton Ale'.[20]

By 1822, Scottish brewers had become noted for the quality of their beers, and A. Colville and A. M. Sandeman wrote in *Dundee Delineated*, 'that at one period there was not a town in Scotland where brewers were more numerous, or ale more famous than in Dundee' and Scottish brewers were producing close to 400 barrels per annum.

By all accounts, the character of Scotch Ale up to 1830 was pale with a mild hop flavour, and in 1837 Roberts wrote *The Scottish Ale Brewer*, which tells us that Scotch Ale was hopped at 4–8lb per quarter (336lbs) of malt, according to the quality of the ale and the season of the year. In winter brewing, 6lb of hops for best ale and 4lb for inferior kinds may be considered a fair estimate.

First worts for high-priced ales

Gravity	Hops lb/qtr	Coppering First charge	Coppering Second charge	Time of coppering
1.095-1.100	10lb	4lb 20 min.	6lb 40 min.	60 min.
1.085-1.090	8lb	4lb 15 min.	4lb 40–50 min.	55–65 min.
1.070-1.080	7lb	2lb 20 min.	5lb 40–50 min.	60–70 min.

Scottish brewers also calculated the quantity of hops to be used by the volume of the brew in barrels. For example, in 1837 John Carter employed 220lb of hops for 60 barrels of wort, and in 1873 Robert Wallace used 336lb of hops to 105 barrels of wort.[46] To convert the quantity of hops per barrel to the rate per quarter, brewers used the following formula:

$$\text{Rate per barrel} = \frac{\text{Rate per quarter x Brewer's gravity of wort}}{\text{Average extract from the grist}}$$

During the nineteenth century, Scotch Ale was to become a most celebrated beer and brought fame and fortune to Scottish brewers at home and abroad. In London during the 1830s, Scotch Ale rivalled Burton Ale and they both retailed at 8½*d* per pint. Wm. Younger's Edinburgh Ale dominated the local market at this time and was described as a potent fluid that almost glued the lips of the drinker together, and was the favourite tipple sold in Dowie's Tavern, a dark windowless howff nicknamed The Coffin situated in Libberton's Wynd that led from the High Street to the Cowgate, and was frequently patronised by the Scottish literati including Ferguson and Burns. Younger's strongest Scotch Ale sold at three pence a bottle and few could consume more than one before they became inebriated!

After the 1840s, Scottish exports became a very lucrative business and Wm. Younger's Edinburgh Ale, Lorimer & Clarks Edinburgh Ale, and Tennent's Scotch Ale, plus Alloa Ale, all colloquially called Scotch Ale, found their way into every corner of the British Empire to quench the thirst of immigrants, their administrators and troops sent there to keep the peace.

However, on occasion the keeping qualities of Younger's Scotch Ale exported to Bombay became more of a liability than an asset, and their Indian agent complained that although the beer was popular it took some eighteen months to fully mature because of its body. Unfortunately, not all of the beer arrived in good condition, and at one time in 1845, Robert's contact in India told him that one consignment arrived in such bad condition that 800 hogsheads were poured into Bombay (Mumbai) harbour![55]

It was during the nineteenth century that brewing in Scotland had evolved into a major industry with output steadily increasing year on year, and in 1850 it produced 500,000 barrels. At this time, Younger's were shipping large quantities of Edinburgh Ale all over the world, and by 1851 they were exporting over 21,000 barrels. In 1854, after a consignment of Wm. Younger's ale arrived in Trinidad, forty casks were sent to Tobago where they were stored for two years before being sold and found to be in excellent condition![34] By 1858, a hogshead of Wm. Younger's export strong ale cost 85/- and at the same time J. & R. Tennent's Double Scotch Ale, India Pale Ale and Brown Stout were becoming popular in India. Only a third of Tennent's exports were in the wood and the bulk was bottled, a product that they were noted for, and Tennent's beers were well regarded in India.

At this time Scotland had 146 breweries, with an annual export market worth £2 million, and Scottish brewers made every effort to ensure that their beer arrived healthy in the Indian subcontinent to secure the best price. Importers in India preferred Scotch Ale brewed during October so that it would arrive in April, which meant that it was considered to be mature within six months.

By January 1876, Wm. Younger was shipping 3,000 barrels of Scotch Ale to India, 'specifically for the troops', and by July the total had reached 8,000 barrels. By 1878, the price per hogshead had reached £8/10*d* or just over 3/- per gallon, but on occasions the supply of ale exceeded demand and the price could drop dramatically, often by as much as 50 per cent. In the worst scenario, the ale had to be stored in the heat of the day and quickly went sour and had to be poured into the sea. Other difficulties were that some unscrupulous importers watered down strong ales but continued to sell the beer as Scotch Ale. There was also some difficulty with dishonest creditors who failed to pay, and there was often the loss of empty casks, which caused huge losses to the exporters.

During the brewery boom of the nineteenth century, Scottish brewers regularly competed at the great Victorian Exhibitions, picking up top awards. In 1866, Ballingall's Pleasance Brewery, Dundee, won gold and silver medals at the Paris Exhibition for their Scotch Ales. In 1869, Wm. Aitcheson, Canongate Brewery, won silver at the Amsterdam Exhibition, silver at London in 1873, and silver at Paris in 1887. In 1873, Wm. Younger received a medal for his sweet stout, which was the fifth medal in five years, and in the same year he was awarded a silver medal at the Moscow Exhibition. Further awards for Ballingall's came in 1878, when they took gold and silver medals at the Paris Exhibition. In 1886, Ballingall's ales from the new Park Brewery beat off competition from the major Scottish brewers to take gold and silver awards at the Edinburgh Exhibition. James Aitken of the Falkirk Brewery competed in the overseas market, winning many honours for his 'high class' ale at the Australian Exhibitions of Sydney in 1879; also, at Melbourne in 1880 and in 1884 at the Calcutta Exhibition, he won acclaim for his Scotch Ale. Further awards came in 1888, at Adelaide, and in 1887, also at Brisbane in 1897. McLay's of Alloa won medals for their oatmalt stout at Vienna in 1894, with further awards for their beers at Paris in 1898 and at Newcastle in 1900.[34] J. & R. Tennent were also active in picking up awards and won gold and top awards at Melbourne in 1880, and at this time they were amongst the leading Scottish brewers in the export trade and further awards for came at Bordeaux and New Zealand in 1882; Venezuela in 1883; Calcutta in 1884; and Chicago in 1893. In 1896, Bell's Brewery gained a prize medal for their ale at the International Concours D'alimentation in Paris, and in 1926 the Bell Brewery was awarded the National Exhibition of Brewers & Allied Trades Prize Medal. At the Brewer's Exhibition in London in 1954, Robert Younger of the St Anne's Brewery, Edinburgh, won a silver medal for his brown ale and a bronze medal for his sweet stout and Old Edinburgh Ale. In 2004, Innis & Gunn won gold medals at the International Beer Competition, plus the prize for the Supreme Champion. In 2007, Harvieston's Bitter & Twisted won the WBA Best Beer Award.

Edinburgh Ale was also brewed in large quantities to satisfy the thirst of gold diggers in Australia, and the emigrant populations in Tasmania and New Zealand. The Edinburgh brewers Wm. Younger and Wm. McEwan both set up a lucrative market in Australasia, and McEwan's had the edge over Younger's due to collaboration with relatives in shipping. The Caribbean market was known as the 'Demerara trade' and regularly imported over 300 hogsheads of Wm. Younger's beer per month. Even in the stifling heat of Trinidad, an importer thought that Edinburgh Ale was excellent, but a little too strong to please in the tropical heat. Tragically, the same importer lost fifty barrels of Edinburgh Ale in a serious fire that razed his premises to the ground.[34]

The USA was also an important market for Scotch Ale, and Younger's representative in St Louis wrote that the most popular beer was the 'Abbey', brewed at the Abbey Brewery and sold in stone champagne-pattern bottles. Also in 1873, Younger's agent in New York reported that sales of Scotch Ale were increasing every year, and despite the difficulties of the American Civil War, cities such as New York, Chicago, Salt Lake City, San Francisco, St Louis and New Orleans were fruitful markets for Scottish brewers. The expats in Canada, Quebec, Toronto and Montreal gave further impetus to the export of Scotch Ale.

Part of the successful export of Scotch Ale was also due to the quality and design of the graceful clipper ships with their pointed bows, long spars and top sails supporting some 32,000-square feet of canvas, which afforded them the ability to harness the trade winds and obtain speeds up to 21 knots.

It was the Scotsman Donald McKay, whose family came from Tain in Ross Shire, who designed twelve of the thirteen clippers that achieved runs of over 400 miles in one day. The distances were huge, sometimes in excess of 12,000 miles, and by keeping the travel time to a minimum they enhanced the prospects of the ale arriving in good condition. In home waters, too, the clipper *Scottish Maid*, built by Alexander Hall of Aberdeen, sailed from Leith to London in a record thirty-three hours. Robert Steele of Greenock was also at the forefront of building the clippers that were so important for the British export trade.

The clippers were primarily built for the tea trade, but beer and other goods were also carried in the hold as ballast, and beer being stored below the waterline was kept cool and fresh. Clipper names such as *The Scotland*, *Ben Vorlich*, *Clan Fraser* and *Lady Agnes Duff* become famous as they plied their ocean trade worldwide. The clipper *Lochiel*, which was built by George Milne, Aberdeen, in 1856, shipped Wm. McEwan's first consignment of 36 hogsheads of No. 3 Ale from Edinburgh to Australia in December 1863. The record-breaking clippers *Thermopylae*, built by Walter Hood & Co, Aberdeen, in 1868, and the *Cutty Sark*, built on the Clyde by Jock Willis Shipping Lines in 1869, became legendary. Today the *Cutty Sark* is the only clipper to survive.

The home market, too, was productive, and the coming of the railways meant that Scottish brewers could reach London and other important markets much quicker than traditional coastal routes. When Scotch Ale was exported to England it was usually brewed at a lower gravity than that for home consumption, but more highly hopped to compete with Burton Ale.

Scotch Ale was typically numbered according to strength, with number one being the strongest down to four the weakest. However, when Wm. Paxton, an Edinburgh ale and porter merchant who had a business in Parliament Close, Perth, sold Edinburgh Ale, he numbered the weakest number one and the strongest number four. The bottles were corked and sealed with coloured wax that also identified the type of beer, typically black for number one, green for number two, brown for number three and yellow for number four.

This is interesting, in that in 1750 Bartholomew Bell founded a brewery in the Pleasance, and was awarded a prestigious medal in 1755 for his Scotch Ale that became known as Black Cork. Bell's beer became celebrated not only in Edinburgh but all over the kingdom, Europe and the East Indies, as the best that the Scotch system of brewing could produce. Also, when French royals came to Scotland as political refugees in 1831, they described Bell's Scotch Ale as 'Scottish Burgundy'.[43] Five years later, and in recognition of this fact, the Edinburgh Society awarded him a prestigious medal. Robert Disher, of the Edinburgh and Leith Brewery, capitalised on the term 'Scottish Burgundy' to describe his 10-Guinea Ale, which sold principally in London and the Home Counties.

Just what special attributes Bell's beer had is not known, but in reality it would have been a typical Scotch Ale of the era, being high gravity, pale in colour, all-malt and well hopped. The name most likely derives from the practice of sealing each bottle with impervious coloured wax, a practice that was also carried out in England.[8] Consequently, there would also be beer known by other colours, but Black Cork is the only one to have any record due to the publicity it acquired during the trial of the notorious Edinburgh thief, Deacon William Brodie, who was by day a Deacon of the Incorporation of Wrights and a much-respected Edinburgh citizen. By night, however, Brodie and his accomplices took part in daring burglaries in the city, until one of the gangs was apprehended and confessed to being a member of the raid on the Excise Office for Scotland.

To escape, Brodie made a bolt for Holland, but was captured and returned to Edinburgh to stand trial. During the hearing, one of the gang told that when they were planning the raid, they met at a friend's house and enjoyed some chicken, herrings and Black Cork. The bemused judge then asked, 'And what is black cork?' The defendant then explained it was Bell's beer, a strong Scotch Ale brewed by Bartholomew Bell at the Pleasance.

In this case, Bell's No. 1 Ale, sealed with black wax, was a popular brew in and around Edinburgh and was bought and sold colloquially by the trade and toper alike as 'Black Cork'. (Of course, we can see that Brown Stout was also dipped in black wax, but the court evidence specifically mentions that Black Cork was Bell's beer and not stout.) Black Cork remained popular until 1837, when the last brewer, Robert Kier, is believed to have died taking the secret recipe to his grave. However, it was in 1837 that Bell's Brewery was taken over by John Jeffrey & Co., and if Black Cork did indeed disappear at this time, the most likely reason for its demise was due the ending of the practice of wax-dipping bottles.

In 1850, Bell's Brewery was taken over by Ritchie & Co., and registered in 1889 when it became part of Edinburgh United Breweries. It was closed down by the Customs & Excise due to brewing irregularities, and in 1935 it again became part of the reformed John Jeffrey & Co. Ltd.[13] In 1894, the celebrated Edinburgh architect P. L. Henderson designed Deacon Brodie's Tavern, which is situated on the corner of the Lawnmarket and Bank Street, in commemoration of William Brodie.

To secure outlets for their beer, many Scottish brewers opened up depots in London, Liverpool and Newcastle, the latter offering a hugely profitable market for low gravity beers often labelled as Best Scotch. The north-east of England

WILLIAM PAXTON,
Edinburgh Ale and London Porter
MERCHANT,
PARLIAMENT CROSS, PERTH.

List of Prices.

INDIA BEER.

	Quarts.		*Pints*	
Table Beer,......	2s. per doz.			
India Beer, ...	4s. ,,	...	*Pints*, 2s. per doz.	Yel. Wax.

EDINBURGH ALE.

	Quarts.		*Pints.*		
No. 1, ...	3s. 0d. per doz	......	1s. 6d. per doz.		Black Wax.
No. 2, ...	3s. 6d. ,,	......	1s. 9d.	,,	Green ,,
No. 3, ...	4s. 0d. ,,	......	2s. 0d.	,,	Brown ,,
No. 4, ...	5s. 6d. ,,	......	2s. 9d.	,,	Yellow ,,

LONDON PORTER.

	Quarts.		*Pints.*		
Porter,............	2s, 6d. per doz.	....			
Stout, ...	3s. 6d. ,,	......	1s. 9d. per doz.		Red Wax.
Brown Stout, ...	4s. 0d. ,,	......	2s. 0d.	,,	Black ,,
Ex. Brown Stout,	5s. 0d. ,,	......	2s. 6d.	,,	Yellow ,,

*** N.B.—Ales ordered to go by his own Carts, delivered Carriage Free to all the Principal Towns in the Neighbourhood.
When Empty Bottles are not given in exchange for full ones, to be charged at 1s. 4d. per Dozen.
Terms Cash.

was a very lucrative market, particularly for east coast brewers. Wm. Younger of Edinburgh dominated the market but Loriner & Clark were also sending 1,000 hogsheads per week by rail to Tyneside. Ballingall's of Dundee also made huge inroads to the north-east, and was well received by the Geordies, and Deuchers of the Lochside Brewery, Montrose, was sending eight sailing ships per week to Newcastle loaded with ales. Alloa brewers were well positioned to market the north-east and also use the Forth and Clyde canal to reach the lucrative markets of Liverpool, Bristol and Dublin. Tennent's of Glasgow were also ideally placed for such markets and the wider empire. The success of the Scottish brewers in the north-east did not go unnoticed, with the Burton brewers who also vied with the Scots in the north-east and Bass in particular making a lucrative market with their own version of Best Scotch.

Whilst one would expect that with such a short coastal or rail link to the English markets the beer would arrive in good condition. However, this was not always the case, and in 1874 a consignment of Wm. Younger's XXP Ale destined for the Crystal Palace, London, was considered to be so bad that it should never have been sent! Also, in 1874 a delivery of Wm. Younger's ale languishing in a cellar in the Strand, London, had been 'working (conditioning) so much that it nearly blew the roof of the tavern!'[34]

None the less, Wm. Younger was very successful in the London market and on one occasion he sent 450 barrels of beer to a single importer in London. Many other Edinburgh brewers were noted for their products, and Wm. McEwan in particular eventually rivalled Wm. Younger. Within the decade of the establishment of his brewery he had secured major contracts in virtually every major city in New Zealand and Australia. Further afield, the town of Alloa, which could boast eight breweries, became so successful and famous for its ales that the town became known as the 'Burton of the North'. Of course, Alloa, like Edinburgh and indeed Burton upon Trent, gained its reputation from the brewing of mild ales, which is ale brewed and sent out exactly as it is brewed.[8]

On the west coast, J. & R. Tennent became well known for the excellent keeping qualities of their beers, which also retained the essential delicate flavour of the hop that was much appreciated in the American market. On 12 October 1854, the *Times* correspondent wrote:

> Large sales of J. & R. Tennent's bottled ale have been made during the last fortnight, at $3.62½ cents to $3.75 cents per dozen, and a sale of about 300 hogsheads of the same brand in wood to arrive at $60 per hogshead. This brand has a larger sale and is more sought after than any other brand on the market, from its being peculiarly adapted to the warm climate of the interior, and is much used in San Francisco.[20]

Such was the popularity of J. & R. Tennent's beers that in the 1880s, whilst they were making plans for lager brewing, they also had to increase production of their Scotch Ale, IPA and stout to meet demand from their export markets. Whilst the brewers of Edinburgh and Alloa tend to get most of the recognition for their beers, it should not be overlooked that Glasgow was also a major brewing centre and at one time had twenty working breweries, and the problem for Glasgow in this respect was that brewing was often overshadowed by tea, tobacco and shipbuilding. As the Glaswegian will tell you, whilst Edinburgh *is* the capital, Glasgow *has* the capital!

The most notable Glasgow brewers were Hugh Baird & Co. of the Great Canal Brewery; Steel & Coulson, Greenhead Brewery; Gillespie & Sons, Crown Brewery; T. Y. Paterson, Petershill Brewery; Gordon & Blair, Home Brewery; MacLachlan's Castle Brewery; and J. & R. Tennent, Wellpark Brewery. Eventually the trade was to become dominated by J. & R. Tennent, who was by the mid-nineteenth century a specialist brewer of pale ale and stout. By 1855, Tennent's was worth a staggering £200,000!

J. & R. Tennent also had a thriving export trade to the English port of Liverpool, which was very lucrative, and also to Bristol and the colonies. Despite the fame of Tennent's lager in the twentieth century, the company still produces a range of high-class beers. An interesting note in the historical records of J. & R. Tennent's tells us that when Bonnie Prince Charlie and his followers rested at Glasgow before their ill-fated adventure into England in 1745, that 'each and every man was refreshed and heartened by the brew of Wellpark'.[4]

In the 1890s, Campbell's De Lux, Old Heavy Scotch Ale, which was only brewed in limited quantities, was exported to Belgium for bottling. 'Campbell's' had a rightfully high reputation for its beers and was granted a Royal Warrant to provide beer to Holyrood Palace by Queen Victoria, and this royal privilege was also granted to Campbell's by Edward VII, George V and George VI. At about the same time, Thomson, Marshall & Co. of the Aulton Brewery, Aberdeen, also had the privilege of suppling beer to Queen Victoria and the Prince of Wales at Balmoral Castle.

In Prestonpans, James Fowler became well known for his 'Celebrated Prestonpans Table Beer', which was possibly the second running from his famous 12-Guinea Crown Ale. In Dundee, the Dudhope Brewery (Neave's) had a representative selling their ales in the Midlands, which was unusual for such a small concern that had a valuation of only £10,000 in 1899.[3]

Despite Scotch Ale becoming superseded by India Pale Ales, the style remained popular and Campbell, Hope and King of the Argyle Brewery, Chambers Street, Edinburgh, started exporting Scotch Ale to Belgium in 1890, and Scottish brewers were now exporting a total of 168,000 barrels, which accounted for one third of the total UK export trade.[29] By 1900, this had risen to 2 million barrels of beer, and in 1907, Wm. Younger was brewing a quarter of all the beer brewed in Scotland.

Until the outbreak of the First World War, Wm. Younger was still exporting

Scotch Ale to England, where it competed with Burton Ale, and they were also exporting Scotch Ale to Belgium, where it was popular at Christmas time. Until 1917, Tsar Nicholas II of Russia and his household enjoyed their own private stock of Younger's XXXS Ale. Even as late as 1950s, Younger's fought a spirited campaign to boost sales of their No. 1 Scotch Ale, 'The King of Ales', in England.

The character of Scotch Ale in the twentieth century was an all-malt beer with a high sweetish terminal gravity and a delicate hop flavour and light hoppy aroma. The original colour of Scotch Ale was typically pale, but later nut-brown for the strongest ale achieved by boiling the first strong wort, rich in the colour precursors, the melanoidins, for up to three hours. Lower gravity Scotch Ales that contained fewer colour precursors were amber in colour.

Scotch Ale was low in carbonation due to long storage times in oak, which allowed the beer to flatten. In the twentieth century, Scotch Ale, like all other brews, underwent reappraisal with a drop in strength being the most obvious, and Younger's No. 1 Scotch Ale, for example, dropped from its 1870s gravity of 1.102 and 10% ABV, to 1.084 in 1923 with an 8% ABV, and by 1955 the gravity was attenuated again to 1.071 with about 6.5% ABV. In the 1990s it was also brewed as McEwan's 70/- and Younger's Tartan Special.[46] The traditional all-malt grist formulation also changed, and we see the use of some roasted barley and crystal malt for colour and flavour with flaked maize and sugar employed for nitrogenous control. This practice would have started after the First World War to compensate for the lower gravity and lighter colour.

Today, Scotch Ale is more commonly found in Belgium rather than its native country, with a character and strength more in keeping with nineteenth-century Scotland. Historically, of course, the ales of yesterday were brewed with high sweet original and final gravities, providing nourishment and energy for an otherwise poor diet.

INDIA PALE ALE

'... good sound beer always fetches its price in India.'
Extract from a letter to W. H. Roberts from a contact in India, dated July 1845

Early in the nineteenth century, Robert Stein was the owner of the Edinburgh and Leith Brewery, but after he became bankrupt in 1819 it was taken over by a partnership, of which Robert Disher was the first managing director from 1820 to 1850, when he became the sole owner. During this time, he fought to end the restrictive trade monopoly and privileges such as setting prices for grain and beer that continued to hinder an already sluggish industry. He is also credited with introducing pale ale into Scotland.[8] In 1821, he brewed Edinburgh Pale Ale, which led to an unprecedented demand for quality barley and malt that in turn brought about a huge change in agriculture and the quality of wort and beer. In 1889, the brewery became part of Edinburgh United Breweries.

Disher's India Pale Ale was the turning point for pale ales in Scotland, and eventually Edinburgh brewers were adding large amounts of calcium sulphate (gypsum) to the mash and copper that was deemed necessary to harden the liquor in a fashion similar to that of Burton upon Trent in an attempt to emulate the success of Allsopp and Bass, Ratcliff & Gretton who were now dominating the export drive to India.

Initially, Scottish India beer was brewed for export to the West Indies, for sale to émigré Scots and planters and merchants in the sugar cane colonies. However, it didn't take the thrifty Scots long to realise the huge financial potential of exporting beer to India, and the brewers of Edinburgh, Alloa and Glasgow in particular, who had ready access to the sea via Leith and by the rivers Forth and Clyde respectively. Much trade was carried out through the East India Company (1600–1873), and some of the export agencies were I. K. Shaw and Messrs Gilander's and Arbuthnot in Calcutta, N. C. Shaw in Madras, and S. S. Miranda in Bombay.

The keeping quality of export beers meant that they travelled well and maintained their condition in extremes of climate. There was much to be gained by only sending out the freshest of beer, as brews arriving in poor condition were sold for a mere song. None the less, the India market became very lucrative, and prior to the 1830s Wm. Younger of the Holyrood Brewery in Edinburgh dominated the market. Thereafter, Meiklejohn's of the Candleriggs Brewery in Alloa, Wm. McEwan of the Fountain Brewery in Edinburgh and J & R Tennent of the Wellpark Brewery in Glasgow also became major players in the field. In particular, Tennent's Strong Ale and India Pale Ale were very popular in India.

The ale was brewed from the palest 'white malt', better known as East India Malt, kilned to 4 EBC° and well dried and not crushed too fine. India Pale Ale had a lighter gravity that was considerably lower than Scotch Ale, and Roberts's investigations tell us that the average gravity for the export beers was 1.068, the average gravity for the home trade was 1.062, and for the cheaper versions of IPA was 1.055. However, the lighter gravity beers were considered to be quite sound, as several of them did a round trip to India and back, and despite crossing the equator four times were considered to be in good condition after eighteen months.

The lighter gravity of IPA was obtained by a mashing heat of 150°F (65°C), which was significantly lower than the typical mash heat of Scotch Ale at 158°F (70°C). The sparging heats ranged from 185°F to 190°F (85–87°C), which is higher than today's value of 168°F to176°F (76–80°C). The gyle was usually split into two worts, with the first being boiled with 8lb of hops per quarter of malt for seventy minutes. The second wort was boiled with another 8lb of hops per quarter for up to two hours. The high hopping rate impregnated the brew with lots of the antiseptic α-acids and maturation mellowed the bitterness and married it up with the residual malt products. We should also take heed of the experiments carried out by Roberts in 1847. He discovered that he could brew an India Pale Ale with considerably less hops than usual and still turn out a brew that remained sound for up to five years! Of course, what wasn't known at the time is that when large amounts of hops are used, less isomerisation of the preservative α-acids takes place, and consequently when fewer hops were used the isomerisation rate increased and so sufficient amounts of α-acids were extracted to preserve the brew. It was also the view of eminent doctors of the day that IPA was a strengthening, exhilarating and wholesome beverage, and they recommended it to their patients!

After coppering, both worts were run down through a hop back to filter the brew before being racked into puncheons (72 gallons) for fermentation. The yeast was pitched at 60°F (15°C), using 2lb of yeast per barrel. In the 1800s, Scottish brewers rarely employed finings as the cool fermentation and storage quickly sedimented the yeast. After the primary fermentation subsided the ale was racked into hogsheads, which were well sulphured to keep them sweet. The quality of the casks for export followed the same strict guidelines as for Scotch Ale, only using the best Baltic oak. When the fermentation was complete 1lb of the finest Kent Golding hops was added to enhance the aroma and the cask bunged down.

Originally, India beers were all-malt, until the government bowed to pressure from the Caribbean sugar cane plantation owners and in 1847 sugar was legalised in brewing. Initially, the Scots made little use of this adjunct, and when sugar was taxed in 1850 there was no great incentive to use it. By 1867, only 8,000 bushels were used. After the sugar tax was abolished in 1880 the character of India Pale Ale started to change, as additions of sugar and cereal adjuncts were considered necessary for nitrogenous control and hence brilliance and microbial stability. By 1886, brewing consumption of sugar in Scotland had risen to 80,000 bushels, which accounted for 4 per cent of the average grist.

During the agriculture depression of the late nineteenth century, farmers complained that the overall Scottish brewers' consumption of sugar was 2,194,050 hundredweights, which was displacing 1,097,015 quarters of malt that was hurting their livelihood. As we can see, sugar was more economical as it provided considerably more extract than malt and the financial advantages are obvious, and by the turn of the century sugar contributed 6 per cent of the grist. By the early twentieth century, McEwan's of Fountainbridge were using 30 per cent flaked maize,10 per cent invert sugar. Not surprisingly, the names of the sugars reflected the names of the sugar cane colonies of the British Empire, and so we come across many such as Fine Mauritius, Havana and Fine Bengal, Jamaica, Egypt and British Guiana. Candy sugar and Golden Syrup were also used, plus Jamaica Molasses and Scotch honey.

In 1885, Wm. Younger of Edinburgh installed 160 union casks in the Abbey Brewery, and 54 union casks in each of No. 1 and No. 2 cellars in the Holyrood Brewery, which was to ensure a product of the highest quality and compete with Burton's brewers. Possibly due to the slow fermenting Edinburgh yeast, the unions did not prove successful and were removed to make room for refrigeration plant and conditioning tanks for high-class Scotch pale ales. Also, in the 1880s, Jeffrey's Heriot Brewery installed some forty union casks and had more success.

By the 1890s, George Younger of Alloa was exporting over 260,000 gallons per annum, which put Bass's 100,000 gallons in the shade, and it is unfortunate that due to mergers and takeovers by the twenty-first century this proud brewing tradition had all but disappeared.

SCOTTISH PORTER

'1806. A. C. and W. Younger; "have engaged a London brewer of great professional ability and they are happy to say that he has succeeded in producing porter that will vie in every respect with the best that can be imported from London."'
To porter dealers, *The Younger Centuries*, David Keir, 1951

The common London porter was noted for its piquant flavour, which was a direct result of contamination due to long storage times in huge vats that were impossible to keep clean. This must be the only example where the flavour of a beer that has gone off turned out to be hugely popular!

The early porters were also strong, with gravities of 1.090 to 1.100, which produced a high alcoholic content that would inhibit the aerobic acetic acid and lactic acid bacteria, as they fail to grow at 6% and 5% alcohol respectively. Therefore, the sourness in the early porters would have come primarily from the acid-producing wild yeast *Brettanomyces* that can continue to respire when other types of yeast are inhibited by the by-products of fermentation. The acid-producing bacterium, *Pediococci*, is also prevalent in sedimented yeast and would have also influenced the flavour. It is also interesting to note that the subtle sub-acid flavour in Guinness comes from lactic acid and not the unacceptable acetic acid.[30] Porter vats and casks were not sulphured after cleaning so that the development of the sub-acid flavour was not affected.

Due to the excreta from wild yeasts and bacteria, porter initially displayed viscosity, mucilage and obnoxious odours, and it might take at least a year's maturation for the beer to clear and the nauseating aromas to dissipate. Also, during maturation the smokiness from the porter malt declines and the sharp acidification mellows and marries up with the residual malt and hop products to produce a harmonious vinous quality.

However, despite the genuine efforts of reputable brewers to maintain high standards, many unscrupulous operators added a range of adulterants, including the poisonous drug Cocculus Indiacus, and Nux Vomica, which contains strychnine, to produce an ersatz porter on the cheap. To avoid the tax on black malt, other substances such as liquorice root, Spanish liquorice and Leghorn juice were added for colour and flavour. Bitter substitutes such as Quassia bark and Fabia Armara (bitter bean) were often used as a substitute for expensively taxed hops. Coriander, caraway, gentian and Grains of Paradise (a type of ginger) acted as flavour enhancers. The latter, according to Morrice, would 'disperse wind and add warmth to the stomach'!

Just how this black vinous bittersweet beer got its name has always been a bit of a mystery, and the most accepted version is that it got its name from the London Street porters who are said to have popularised it. Such an idea has been around for a long time, and it is rather easy to link the beer 'porter' with that of street porters, but such a notion lacks evidence.

The author previously put forward the theory that the name derived from the similarities with the fortified wine port.[1] However, after further research a more credible reason for the name might come from an old Scottish weaving term 'porter', which donated a certain number of threads forming a section of warp. The warp threads are those that are permanently fixed and run the length of the loom, as opposed to the weft threads that are delivered crosswise by the shuttle. Hornsey tells us that in London in the 1720s there was a habit of mixing mild and stale beer with a portion of twopenny, and this was called 'three-threads', although some hostelries were also advertising four-threads and five-threads, with the beer coming from up to five separate casks, and immediately we can see a connection with the weaving term 'porter' for the threads forming the warp and the beer called three-, four- or five-threads.[29]

The weavers were artisans who operated a skilled trade, and it is plausible that when they were chatting amongst themselves in the workplace and in taverns that they would simply refer to the beer called 'three-threads' as a 'porter'? Surely, others within earshot would also pick up the jargon and that 'porter' would become a popular expression for three-threads in the taverns where it was sold, and so the general public would quickly catch on to the expression and, consequently, the term 'porter' would become viral?

In the *London and Country Brewer*, we come across another brown beer from the same era that was called 'stitch', which was made from the first long runnings from a stout mash, and as 'stitch' is also a nickname for a tailor we can again see a further connection with the weaving trades. Therefore, the most logical conclusion we can draw from this is that the naming of porter and stitch beers does have its origins in the weaving trades and not that of street porters.

With the rise of the common brewers in the eighteenth century, porter brewing became very lucrative and required huge vats to store and mature this popular beer, which inevitably led to one-upmanship amongst the major English brewers, and it became a matter of prestige to see who could build the biggest vat. Such competition did not go unnoticed among the media, and on 1 April 1785, *The Times* reported that Meux & Co., Liquorpond Street, Gray's Inn Lane, London, were building a huge vat, 'which exceeds all credibility', capable of holding 20,000 barrels (720,000 gallons or 5,760,000 pints!) of porter.

The building of such a vat was a huge undertaking, and each oak stave was 30ft in length by 5–6ft wide and 3ft thick. The vat had a width of 69ft and to hold all of this together required about 25–30 enormous hoops, each of them 217ft in circumference and weighing up to 2–3 tons! The vats were usually built upon a raised timber platform supported on cast-iron or wood pillars, some 10ft high, which allowed the porter to be casked by gravity and also allowed storage and a working area below.

The enthusiasm for building such enormous vats waned when a fairly modest-sized one containing 3,550 barrels collapsed at Henry Meux's Horse Shoe Brewery, London, on 17 October 1814, killing eight people.

The cause of the disaster is said to have been a hoop falling off, but if we look at the construction of the vat, they were certainly strong enough to withstand the loss of one hoop. However, the question remains: how does a hoop fall off a vat? In reality they don't, but they might slip and I think this provides a clue to what might have happened.

If the vat in question was partially empty, the timber at the top would dry out somewhat and a small degree of shrinkage would be enough to allow the top hoop, which might have weighed as much as two tons, to slip and slam onto the hoop below and dislodges it. Now two 2-ton hoops slam onto the next hoop and dislodge it; now three hoops weighing 6 tons slip and slam into the next hoop; and so on, with an ever-increasing weight and speed. The rapid domino effect of the falling hoops severely weakens the integrity of the vessel and the enormous weight of 3,550 barrels of porter forces the staves apart, producing a huge fountain.

Also, and in conjunction with the above, the tremendous shock of the kinetic energy produced by the enormous falling weight of 60–90 tons of the collapsing hoops shattered the timber platform and caused the cast-iron columns to disintegrate and the whole structure and vat collapsed, triggering a powerful surge of porter that caused death and destruction in its wake.

It should also be considered that had the platform not collapsed, it is unlikely that the cascade of porter escaping from the separated staves would have caused the damage reported in the press. Whilst the flood would have been great, it would be somewhat controlled by the thinly separated oak staves held fast by the band of hoops at the base. However, as the staging collapsed and the huge vat toppled over, breaking up as it did so, the huge tidal wave of some 127,800 gallons of porter and floating staves caused mayhem in its wake. I would also question what is written about the position of storehouse clerk, George Crick, when the vat 'burst'. He is reputed to have been standing next to the vat, and coincidentally he just happened to be holding the report that he had written about a hoop previously falling of a vat, and yet when the calamity occurred, and despite the catastrophe and deaths that ensued, he was unharmed.

Of course, tall, narrow vats were slightly tapered so that the hoops could be well driven, which adds to the problem of how a hoop falls off, or indeed slips. However, the larger vats of 66m in circumference were by all accounts straight-sided, and so the theory fits. We also have to consider the weight of the hoops to appreciate that they were so heavy that they were not manually lifted into place, and so block and tackle must have been used. In the case of the straight-sided vats, the hoops would have been heated to expand the metal and cooled when lowered into place to shrink them tightly around the vat.

If the above theory isn't porter-tight, then there has to be some reason for the staging to collapse, because the theory that a hoop fell off a vat causing the catastrophe simply doesn't stand up to rational scrutiny.

Perhaps the English porter vat catastrophe weighed heavily on the conscience of Scottish brewers and the size of porter vats remained modest, typically about 300 barrels. None the less, English porter was popular in Scotland and publicans in Perth had a reciprocal arrangement when sloops and schooners took the famed Tay Salmon to London and brought back porter. The wholesale cost was 50/- to 60/- a hogshead and typically sold at 4p a pint. However, imported porter could not compete with small beer or the stronger Scotch Ale, which was the fare of the poor and the rich respectively.

The canny Scot, however, was keen to capitalise on this fashionable drink, but early Scottish Porter was inferior to

The porter vat calamity.

imported porter and attempts to put this right resulted in Scottish brewers recruiting London and Dublin porter brewers. The earliest attempt to do this took place in Edinburgh in 1752, when Thomas Cleghorn enlisted a London porter brewer to ensure that his product matched the best London Porter.[20] However, the soft well water of the west coast was considered to be better for the production of dark beers, and porter brewing commenced in Glasgow about 1760. Contemporary opinion had it that the quality of Glasgow porter fell far short of the London article.

If Scottish brewers were enlisting London porter brewers to produce an authentic article, did the brews contain any of the obnoxious ingredients that found their way into London porter? Scottish porters were brewed with pale, brown, amber and black malts, but it is also known that McLay's of Alloa

BLACK BULL INN,

11 KIRKGATE,

Market Cross, Perth.

WINES and SPIRITS of the finest quality.

LONDON PORTER.

EDINBURGH ALES.

R. M'CULLOCH,

PROPRIETOR.

EVERY CONVENIENCE FOR FARMERS.

were using the innocuous liquorice (Sugarallie) and linseed at the turn of the twentieth century.

In 1763, the Glasgow brewers Peter Murdoch and James Warroch established the Anderston Brewery in the city, although the Edinburgh brewers John and William Cunningham managed it initially. By the 1770s, they had begun to brew porter, with much competition coming from John Struthers who was brewing at the Gallowgate Brewery. To improve on the quality of their product and gain the competitive edge over their competitors, Murdoch and Warroch recruited the brewing skills of Nathaniel Chivers in 1775.

Chivers had been previously schooled in the great porter breweries of London and Dublin, and it was to be his task to improve on the quality of local porter in order to compete with the imported product. Also, by brewing an authentic article they would secure an advantage over their close rival, John Struthers. In order to protect their investment in Chivers and beat off rivals, he was contracted to produce porter with the same flavour and keeping qualities as London porter and, most importantly, the contract also forbade him from divulging the techniques of porter brewing to other brewers in and around Glasgow, under the penalty of 100 guineas.

Chivers's brewing skills earned him about £25 per month, a huge sum in those days. However, the following year Murdoch and Warroch had probably learned enough about porter brewing and, seeing the huge saving of £300 a year, decided to dispense with the services of Chivers, and he was dismissed and handed his fare back to London. Chivers, no doubt, would have felt badly let down and aggrieved by his dismissal. On studying his contract, he realised that it was not as 'porter-tight' as first thought and there was no legal obstacle to prevent him brewing in competition against his old employers. Therefore, instead of taking the long arduous coach journey to London, he entered into a partnership with John Struthers in the Gallowgate.

This move was, however, to be his undoing, and when word got around that Chivers was brewing porter at the Gallowgate Brewery, Murdoch and Warroch had no alternative but to take the matter to law. The fact that Chivers had entered a partnership, rather than brew on his own, broke the spirit of the contract, and Murdoch and Warroch obtained an interdict that forbade him from revealing the secrets of porter brewing to their rivals.[15, 29, 35] However, by the time the interdict was enforced Struthers had acquired the secrets of porter brewing, although Murdoch and Warroch remained the dominant porter brewers in Glasgow.

With such expertise from the skilled London and Dublin porter brewers, the Scots quickly turned the tables on their English rivals, and by 1785 Scottish Porter exports to England matched the imports of London Porter. Meanwhile, in Edinburgh, William Younger and Company had built up a thriving porter trade but were cautious about the quality of their product, and as a safeguard hired a London porter brewer of 'great ability' in 1806.

The principal porter brewers in Scotland during the period 1752 to 1806 were as follows:

Thomas Cleghorn, Edinburgh
Murdoch & Warroch, Anderston Brewery, Glasgow.
John Struthers, Gallowgate, Glasgow
Gabriel Richardson, Dumfries
Alexander Young's College Brewery, Elgin
William Gillies, Brechen Brewery
Robert Stein, Canongate, Edinburgh and Glasgow
William Black, Devanha Brewery, Aberdeen
William Younger, Edinburgh
Robert Meiklejohn, Candleriggs Brewery, Alloa
Archibald Campbell & Co, Argyle Brewery, Edinburgh

Around 1812, the quality of Scottish porter was so good that many considered the importation of English porter to be unnecessary. During the 1820s, Scottish porter was also categorised in shillings, and the cellars of Robert Stein's Edinburgh brewery contained 40 barrels of 115/- porter, 433 barrels of 90/- porter, 16 barrels of 80/- porter, 4 barrels of 40/- porter and 30 barrels of 30/- porter. The total value of this stock amounted to some £2,301, a substantial sum of money in the early nineteenth century. Also, his Glasgow brewery cellared 7,000 barrels of porter and had eight large porter vats holding 300 barrels.

With the increase of ales and porter coming from the small provincial brewers, the City of Edinburgh slapped a tax of 2*d* per pint on all imported beers. Wm. Black's Aberdeen Porter in particular was a big seller in Edinburgh, and in 1817 he was pursued through the courts by the Edinburgh authorities for non-payment of the 2*d* tax.

By 1820, the exportation of Scottish porter to England amounted to 16,944 barrels, and in 1821, Archibald Campbell of the Argyle Brewery became the leading brewer exporting porter to England.

In *A Practical Treatise on Brewing*, 1835, Scotsman William Black tells a sad but funny tale about a death that occurred in a porter brewery. Apparently, a Dutch house was in the practice of getting whole gyles of porter brewed for them by one of the great porter houses in London. On one occasion, one of their clerks was in London at the time of brewing and went to see the process. He unfortunately, poor fellow, tumbled into a copper full of boiling wort, and before he could be got out again, he was boiled to death! The gyle of beer was sent over to Holland and turned out to be very good! The next batch sent, however, did not turn out so well, and the Dutch House complained of it, saying it did not have the same flavour as the preceding gyle. The answer returned by the London House was that they had no means of giving them exactly the same flavour unless they would send them over another Dutchman![11]

By 1841, Wm. Younger had so much faith in his product that he was shipping his full-bodied XXXP Export Porter to England and the Empire. About the same time, Robert Meiklejohn of the Candleriggs Brewery in Alloa enlisted the Scotsman Robert Ferguson, who was a porter brewer in London, to improve the quality of his product. By this time porter had become the true national drink, and eventually the international beer as it was brewed and consumed throughout the United Kingdom, Scandinavia, the Baltic states, Poland, Holland and much of the Empire.

By the 1860s, J. & R. Tennent of Glasgow were very successful brewers of porter and stout, brewing some 28,000 barrels annually. Also, during the 1860s Ballingall's of Dundee rivalled the best Scottish porter brewers and matured their porter in vats, containing up to 250 barrels, in the old Pleasance Brewery.

Porter was a godsend for Scottish brewers exporting to India, as in one sense it couldn't go off, or acid, a fate that often befell Scotch Ale and India beers. A daily pint of porter was issued to the troops prior to training, which no doubt encouraged the malingerer to muster. It was also considered to be a tonic against cholera and many Asian ills, and was a regular medicine doctored in the sick bay, which might have been a good excuse for reporting sick!

In Scotland, by the late nineteenth century, the popularity of porter slowly declined. In the Scottish Wine, Spirit and Beer Trades review of September 1887, it was stated that many brewers complained of the difficulty of securing any considerable sale for black beers, and there was no doubt that the whole trend of the brewing trade was to develop itself in the direction of light bitter ales of low alcoholic strength and that of delicate flavour, created by judicial hopping with high-class materials.[35]

Due to the severe restrictions introduced by the British Government on roasting malts and barley during the First World War, to save on energy, plus the trend away from black beers in particular, porter had all but disappeared from the market by 1918.

SCOTTISH LAGER

'It is a beer that not only drinks well but will keep well in any climate. No matter how much the bottle may be shaken or what the temperature may be, this lager will remain clear and bright, a pleasure to drink, pure and wholesome.'

Tennent's lager by the *Victualling Trades Review*, January 1908

In the 1820s and 1830s, Gabriel Sedlmayr of the Spaten Brewery, Munich, travelled throughout Europe, England and Scotland, learning the secrets of brewing in each country. In Scotland he visited Alloa and Edinburgh, and whilst in Edinburgh he stayed at the Calton Hill Brewery, 26 North Back Canongate, a brewery run by John Muir and sons from 1830 until 1916. Muir taught Sedlmayr the techniques of Scottish brewing, and when he returned to Munich in 1835 he took a sample of Muir's yeast with him and had several attempts at brewing Scotch Ale. It is a safe bet that some of the yeast infected the wooden vessels in the Spaten Brewery. Sedlmayr also enlightened Muir about how Munich beer was brewed and he sent him a sample of Munich yeast, and that year Muir became the first British brewer to brew lager bier.[49]

At around the same time, Jacob C. Jacobson of the Carlsberg Brewery had undertaken several visits to Europe to further his knowledge of brewing. In 1845 he also visited Sedlmayr's Spaten Brewery in Munich, where he was tutored in the techniques of bottom fermentation, and before he returned home Sedlmayr supplied his protege with copious amounts of yeast. Legend has it that during the long journey home he kept the yeast under his stove-pipe hat to keep it cool. The yeast survived, and in 1846 Jacobsen was successfully brewing Munich lager beer. However, the beer was plagued by periodic infections, and due to the experiments carried out by Emil Christian Hansen, the Munich yeast was found to have a mixed population of wild yeast that produced mixed results. It was not until 1879–83 that a pure bottom yeast culture was isolated at the Carlsberg laboratories. Whether or not Jacobsen reciprocated an exchange of the new pure yeast with his old master, the Spaten Brewery did not brew Bavaria's first pale lager until 1894. It is a whimsical thought indeed that the pure yeast isolated by Hansen might well have originated in Edinburgh.

In the meantime, Wm. Younger of Edinburgh dominated the huge and lucrative market of Empire for draught ales, whilst J. & R. Tennent of Glasgow monopolised the overseas trade with their bottled beer. However, by the mid-1880s British brewers found it increasingly difficult to access foreign trade due to the increasing competition from Bohemian, German and Dutch brewers.

By this time continental brewers were producing paler, lighter and more refreshing beers that were much more suited to the warmer overseas markets. Since 1875, the Dutch in particular had mastered the pasteurisation techniques necessary to allow them to export their lightly hopped sparkling refreshing beers to India, the East Indies and South America, and Heineken brewers could boast: 'our bottled beer remains in very good condition for six months or more'. In Rio de Janeiro, Brazil, a Wm. Younger importer demanded that in order to suit the hot climate their beer must be frothy, pale in colour but not too bitter.

The trend was now steadily towards lighter-gravity beers with a refined hop flavour, which encouraged companies such as Bischoffe & Co. of Glasgow and Gamle Carlsberg Lager Beer Import Co. of Leith to import Scandinavian and German lager beers. The Kaiser Lager Beer Co. Ltd of Niedermendig on the Rhine also set up an agency in Scotland to take advantage of the increasing popularity of lager beer.

Scottish brewers were now forced to reconsider their position with regards to the brewing of lager beer. However, when British brewers began producing lager in a big way, they made the mistake of thinking that they had to exactly emulate the continental decoction mashing process, which Lloyd Hind described as, 'A masterpiece of empiricism.' At this time British brewers were importing large amounts of six-rowed barleys from abroad, and so it was probably a natural step to adopt decoction mashing; and of course, they were not to know that good lager wort can be obtained from well-modified two-rowed lager malt using programmed mashing or a rising temperature infusion mash.

The second Scottish brewer to take up the challenge was Wm. Younger of Edinburgh, and a series of lager-brewing trials began during 1879 under the watchful eye of chief chemist Dr William McGowan and head brewer George Stenhouse. Such was the success of the initial trials that plans were made for full lager production in 1880. Younger's were keen to produce a high-quality brew, and as their experiment with unions was unsuccessful, they were removed from the Holyrood brewery and lauter-tuns, an ice-house and lagering cellars installed in their place. Younger's also sought the help of

Carlsberg lager brewers in Copenhagen, who provided them with know-how and more importantly their bottom-fermenting yeast. This yeast, however, was not, as commonly believed, *Saccharomyces carlsbergensis*, the strain that was isolated and cultivated by Hansen in the Carlsberg laboratories in early 1880s, as it was not used for the first time in the Old Carlsberg Brewery until 12 November 1883.

In the spring of 1880 lager brewing started in earnest, and a German brewing consultant was appointed in late 1881. Such was the initial enthusiasm that Younger's considered building a lager brewery in London, but during the first four years only forty-odd small-scale brews had taken place, and by 1885 lager brewing had ceased at Holyrood. It has been speculated that part of the reason for the cessation of lager brewing was that whilst the well water at the Holyrood brewery was good for top fermenting ales, it was not ideal for pale lager beer.

Meanwhile, the soft water of the west coast suited lager brewing to a 'T' and J. & R. Tennent began brewing lager trials in 1885. To ensure a high-quality authentic product, they enlisted the eminent Danish scientist Dr Emil Westergaard and German brewmaster Jacob Klinger, to supervise the brewing. The first batch of Tennent's all-malt 'Pilsner-type' lager was brewed during 1887 and the bottled version was labelled 'J. & R. Tennent's Munich Beer'. Contemporary opinion was that the lager beer fared very favourably against the imported product.

At this time Tennent's were hugely successful brewers of pale ale and stout, but with the successful launch of lager beers there was a need for more space and a decision to build a brewery especially for lager brewing on the adjacent Wellpark was taken in 1889, the same year that Tennent's lager took top prize at the Chicago World Fair. The contract to build the new brewery went to the German firm Reidinger of Augsburg, and the brewery quite naturally was designed on German principles. Keen on producing an authentic product, Tennent's also employed Bavarian coopers to build the huge maturation casks in the lagering cellars. The brewery was completed in 1891 and lager brewing still takes place at Wellpark to this day. Interestingly, Tennent's also experimented with lager stout, which was to be brewed for the winter months.

The success of J. & R. Tennent's lager beer did not go unnoticed by the other Scottish brewers, and John Jeffrey & Co. Ltd of the Heriot Brewery, Roseburn Street, Edinburgh, started brewing lager beer in 1902. Conscious of the need for authenticity, he too engaged a German brewmaster, Jacob Klinger, to supervise the brewing.

The local product was kept for three months before sale and the stronger export version required lagering for up to ten months to fully ripen. However, Jeffrey's lager brewing was somewhat disappointing, with sales fluctuating between 100 and 300 barrels per week, and with so much capital spent on establishing the product it had an adverse reaction on their regular trade. None the less, lager brewing was now established in Scotland and other brewers took to the lauter tuns.

In 1906, the Edinburgh brewers M. C. Cameron & Co. North British Brewery, Canongate, were brewing a lager called

'Pioneer Brand', and whilst home sales were disappointing, sales to the Empire, particularly Africa and India, were more fruitful. However, by 1911 the company was in trouble and went into receivership, and John Calder of the Shore Brewery, Alloa, was brought in to rescue the business. In 1922, the business was acquired by Wm. Murray & Co. Ltd, Duddingston.

In 1911 the Burton brewers, Allsopps, fell into the hands of the receivers, which was a spectacular fall from grace from a pinnacle of brewing 60,000 barrels of lager in 1877, and John Calder of the Shore Brewery in Alloa was brought in to revive the business. In 1913, John Calder was invited onto the board of Allsopps. After the First World War, Archibald Arrol of the Alloa Brewery was in difficulty, and John Calder was inducted into the management board. In 1921, Calder closed the Shore Brewery and relied on Arrol's to supply his tied estate. At the same time, he transferred the redundant Allsopps lager plant from Burton to the Alloa Brewery, where it later produced Allsopps British Lager that became a brand leader at home and abroad under the supervision of Swedish brewmeister Joseph Lundgren.[38]

In 1927, John Calder started to brew lager, and by the 1930s it became popular in Watney's tied estate. Eventually the lager was brewed by Graham & Co. at Archibald Arrol's Alloa Brewery, and it became well known as Graham's Golden Lager, one of the most widely distributed beers brewed in Scotland. Up to 1934, Arrol's lager was also produced. After Grahams were taken over by Ind Coope, the name changed for a time to 'Graham's Continental', and then to 'Graham's Skoll', and eventually in 1958 just 'Skoll', a beer that went on to be the leading brand in the 1960s. Ind Coope also produced Jaguar Lager.

The grist for Arrol's lager in 1934 is interesting, and consisted of Californian malt, Tunisian malt, Auchak malt, Australian malt, English malt and flaked rice. Added to the copper were malt extract and Martinaeus sugar, plus Martinaeus sugar for primings. The hop grist consisted of Auscha hops (a hop from the Auscha region in Czechoslovakia with a similar delicate flavour and aroma to Saaz), Styrian Goldings and Fuggle. The liquor treatment consisted of 10lb of gypsum, which was added to 2,689 gallons of liquor.

In 1935, J. & R. Tennent introduced the first canned lager in Brasso shaped cans, and as lager sales increased, they introduced their 'Special' lager at 9% ABV and 'Breaker' malt liquor. Drybrough's of Craigmillar, Edinburgh, started brewing a lager called Scottish Pride Lager, and Wm. Murray, also of Craigmillar, brewed 'Murray's Lager'. George Younger of Alloa brewed 'Ship Brand' lager, the name possibly coming from the firm's success in the export market with their beers and stouts.

In 1955, Scottish Brewers produced McEwan-Younger's 'MY Scotch Lager' that was brewed and bottled at the Red Tower Brewery (later the Royal Brewery) in Manchester. In 1955, Tennent's became the first British brewer to adopt 16oz cans, and in 1963 they produced the first British 'keg' lager and introduced it as 'The Blond in the Bar!'

In 1961, Guinness formed a consortium of brewers consisting of Mitchells & Butlers, Courage and Scottish & Newcastle to sell their recently introduced lager beer called 'Harp', which was of course the Guinness trademark. Initially Harp was a bottled beer, but in 1965 it became available in keg and found a ready market in Scotland, where it was often served with a dash of lemon juice. It was described on television advertising as 'Harp stays Sharp'! The Guinness consortium also built a lager plant at the Scottish & Newcastle brewery in Fountainbridge to meet the demand for lager in Scotland. In the 1970s, Usher/Vaux were brewing 'Norseman Lager', which might have been the same brew as their Golden Lager that sold in the north-east.

In 1976, Scottish & Newcastle Breweries introduced 'McEwan's Lager', which fell out of favour by 2003, but it was re-launched in 2008 as McEwen's Lager Cold and Younger's produced Kestrel Lager.

The first microbrewery in Scotland to brew lager was Harvieston Brewery, at Alva, who produced 'Schiehallion Lager' in the 1980s. Innis & Gunn introduced Golden Oat Lager brewed with naked (huskless) golden oats, and went on to win gold twice at the prestigious Monde Selection.

Today, Tennent's lager is the bestselling pint in Scotland, taking 60 per cent of the lager market.

TRADITIONAL SCOTTISH DRAUGHT BEER

'The beer that's working when the barman isn't.'
An early 1980s billboard advertisement for McEwan's cask 80/- Ale.

Historically, beer for immediate consumption was stillaged on the gantry, but when new towns were built with basements it became common for beer to be stored in the cool cellar. Of course, whilst the beer kept better, the immediate problem was getting beer from the cellar to the bar, and initially this task was carried out by 'pot boys' who were kept busy scurrying up and down rickety stairs. This too was problematic and led to the development of the beer engine, or hand pump, invented by Joseph Bramah in 1785, which came into widespread use. The hand pump remained popular until the Scots invented the air-pressure system (water engine) as a means of raising beer to the bar.

One of the earliest references to the use of air pressure to raise beer in Scotland comes from a talk given to the London Section of the Institute of Brewing in 1925 by James Auld of Thomas Usher & Son. In his talk he stated that air pressure was used in Scotland from 1814. Thomas Usher & Son were at this time brewing at the Cowgate Brewery, Edinburgh, and in 1860 the business moved to the Park Brewery, 106 St Leonard's Street, where it remained until closure by Allied Brewers in 1981.

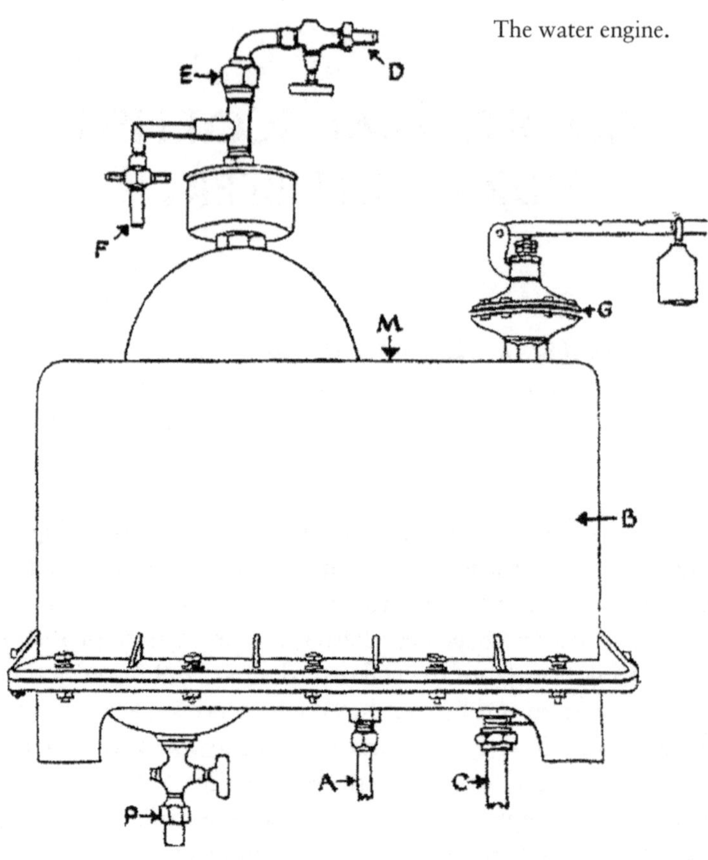

The water engine.

However, it was not until the 1870s that an air-pressure hydraulic system using mains water pressure came into regular use in raising beer from the cellar. One of the earliest water engines to come on the scene was the 'Albany', produced by John McGlashan at Albany Works, 15 Cathedral Lane, Glasgow, which was described as, 'A hydro-pneumatic beer self-raising engine.' The Albany worked in a fashion similar to a lavatory cistern, and mains water enters the cast-iron casing at 'A' via port holes in a gun-metal slide casing, which initially lies clear of the incoming water. One end of the slide casing is designed to block the water inlet port and the other end covers the discharge port 'C'. As the water level rises, so too does the 'ballcock' that is linked mechanically to the slide valve, and the air in the chamber is forced out into the air lines 'D' and into the cask at a typical pressure of 15psi.

As the water reaches a pre-determined level, the ballcock trips a balanced hammer that opens the slide valve, which covered the discharge port 'C', allowing the water to discharge to the Gents, and at the same time closes the inlet port 'A' and shuts off valve 'E', thereby retaining the air pressure in the beer line and cask.

As the water is discharged, air is drawn into the casing through a non-return valve 'F', and at the same time the ballcock falls until the casing is empty and the balanced hammer is tripped back into its original position, and the slide moves to cover the outlet and open the inlet ports. This cycle is automatically repeated until the pre-determined pressure is reached. When the tap on the counter is opened, there is an immediate drop in pressure in the system and a rubber diaphragm 'G' responds and allows the control valve to admit a further volume of mains water to re-establish pressure equilibrium.[42]

The water engine stood the test of time and the head brewer at Usher's, John Miller, wrote in the 1950s: 'several machines in use today are over forty years old and are still giving excellent service, thus proving the efficiency and soundness of the original conception'.[41]

Another ingenious machine was The Bruce, Beer and Liquor Raising Machine, which was simpler in operation. It was made by Archibald Bruce's Works, Cathedral Street, Glasgow, and was constructed of gun metal that made it more durable and also took up less space than the Albany, and it was considered to be ornamental enough to be situated on the bar counter or in the window. Another advantage over other water engines was that the water could be shut off when the device was not in use. The Bruce became the most popular beer engine in Glasgow.

By the turn of the twentieth century, McCallum & Harris introduced a new concept of water engine that included an intermediate air storage cylinder, which regulated the flow of air from the water engine to the cask. During the 1930s, the Laidlaw water engine was produced, and the only difference between it and the Albany was a more effective trip valve that made the engine more efficient. In 1946, Gaskell & Chambers produced the Dalex water engine, which was wall-mounted with a circular viewing window and could deliver a constant pressure of 12–40psi (0.8–2.7 Bar). The last water engine to be made was the Atall, produced by Aitken & Allen of Edinburgh in the 1950s.[42] Aitken (At) Allan (All): the Atall!

The Edinburgh branch of the Campaign for Real Ale lists the last pubs in the city to use a water engine in the 1980s, which were: the Castle Inn, Dirleton; Jimmy Muir's, Sandport Place; Mather's Bar, Broughton Street; Oxford Bar, Young Street; the Piershill Tavern, Piershill Place; the Bull, Cowgate; and the Diggers on Henderson Terrace.

Due to new water regulations designed to cut down on waste, electric air compressors became common. One of the earliest electric air compressors was the Scottish Champion, ironically produced by the American 'Century Electric Company' of St Louis! This engine also had the advantage of individually regulating the pressure to a number of casks. In the 1890s, Bishop & Babcock of Cleveland in Ohio produced two efficient air compressors called the Big Wonder and Little Wonder, and Bowman & Webster of Aberdeen imported these. During the 1930s gas engines were introduced.

Unlike the practice in English pub cellars where casks are stillaged on their bellies, Scottish publicans sit the cask on its end head. This practice came about after the introduction of the air-pressure system, which caused leakage through the cask staves on the bilge (pitch) when the cask was stillaged horizontally. Casks in Scotland were also fitted with an extra hoop to cope with the extra pressure.

After the beer has matured and cleared bright, the extractor is fitted through the tap keystone. The extractors have a venting cock similar to the long syphons used for lager beer on the continent, and the beer has to be vented before air pressure is applied to force the beer to the tall fount on the bar counter. The top air pressure of this method helps the beer retain a degree of valuable CO_2 conditioning in solution, which helps prevent oxygenation, and despite the constant presence of deleterious air above the beer, the brew remains sound throughout its short shelf life.

We should also take note of the comments in *Licensed Houses and their Management*, written by a brewer referring to the Scottish method of drawing beer. 'There is much to be said for this system, as the air pressure has the effect of holding the natural gas in the beer and so ensuring a good condition when served'.

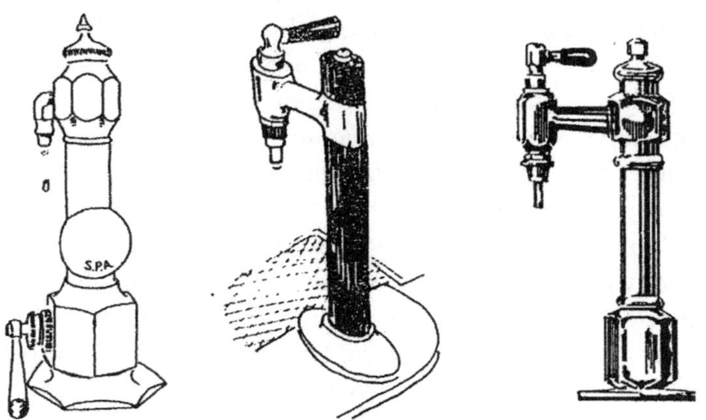

The Albany, the Dalex and Aitken tall founts.

When the Campaign for Real Ale started in 1972, they decided to look at the Scottish method of dispense, and initially decided to overlook the air pressure system and include pubs serving cask beer by air pressure in the *Good Beer Guide*.

However, in 1977, Truman's introduced a cask beer called Tap Bitter that was served by air pressure, and with a degree of indignation the National Executive of CAMRA decided that air pressure was unacceptable in England, claiming that the beer could not 'breathe', and outlawed the system. In order to provide a level playing field, the National Executive also banned Scottish pubs using air pressure from the *Good Beer Guide*! Not surprisingly, the Scottish branches, which were formed in 1975, were hugely offended and stated that unless there was to be a change of heart, they would go it alone. After many debates an emergency conference allowed the use of air pressure, but gave discretion to branches whether or not to allow public houses using air pressure to appear in the *Good Beer Guide*.[50] Of course, ignorance is bliss, and people who hold such ill-informed views have obviously never tasted a pint of Scottish beer drawn in the traditional manner.

One reason why the Scots invented the water engine might be that Scottish legalisation stated that a beer must be served above the counter and in full view of the customer, something that a hand pump fails to do. Therefore, it became necessary to mount a tall tap on the bar counter that became known as 'counter fountains', which became abbreviated to 'founts', although the 'u' is silent.

With an understanding of how the tall fount works the reader will more appreciate why the beer becomes soft on the palate and acquired a tight creamy head. As can be seen in the diagram, the fount has two beer lines: one comes direct from the cask and the other from the return tray. To facilitate this, the tap has one opening on one side from which beer is drawn direct from the cask, and on the other side there are two openings, one lines up directly to the cask outlet and the other lines up with the line coming from the return tray.

The air pressure in the cask propels the beer to the fount, and when the tap is as right angles to the fount pillar, all openings are shut off. However, when the publican draws the first pint of the day, he pours it into the return tray. He does this by turning that tap handle backwards, which does seem unconventional but this action lines up the opening with the beer line from the cask. When serving a customer, the same action is repeated, and as the inevitable frothing and fobbing takes place it is collected in the return tray. As the level in the return tray rises it is reduced by turning the tap forward and it now lines up the two openings with the cask and the return tray. As the beer flowing from the cask passes over the opening from the return tray, it creates an area of low pressure. This in turn

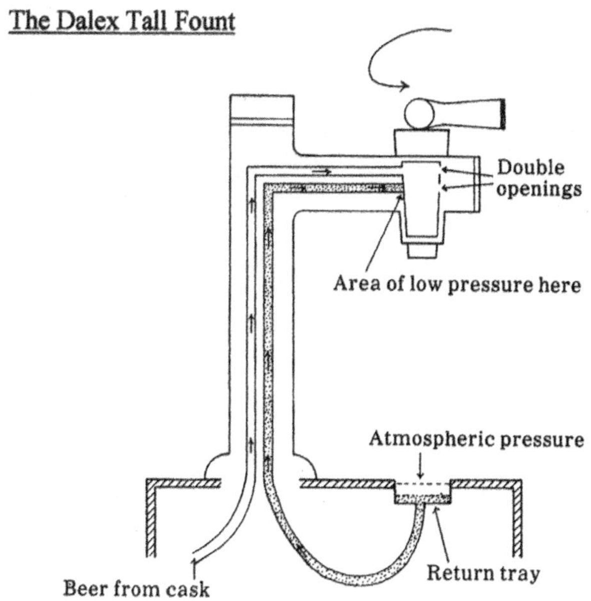

allows atmospheric pressure pressing down on the surface of the beer in the return tray and forces it to the tap, where it becomes mixed with the beer from the cask. As the beer flows throughout the circuit, it loses CO_2 and becomes softer and a degree of aeration takes place. As air is superior to CO_2 and nitrogen in creating foam, the end result is a soft pint with a tight creamy head.

Due to the recycling of the beer, the law stated that a clean glass must be used each time to avoid the beer becoming contaminated with someone else's bugs! With the introduction of recent hygiene regulations for the above reasons the tall fount has been outlawed and, sadly, events have turned full circle and the tall fount has largely been superseded by the hand pull, which has now become the symbol for cask-conditioned ale.

BOTTLED BEER

'The advance in sales of bottled beers for some years past has been very remarkable, and under normal conditions of supply these form a large part of the trade in almost all licensed premises.'

Extract from *Licensed Houses and their Management*, 1923

Bottled beer has been around in Scotland since the seventeenth century, when a glass and bottling trade was established in North Leith for the brewing trade by the enterprising Sir James Stansfield in 1679. However, it was only with the demand for fresh-keeping beer in the eighteenth century that bottled beer started to become popular among the middle classes, who did not wish to visit smelly dingy taverns and ale houses. Many of the early bottles were actually of stone manufacture, and being labour intensive they were very expensive. Companies such as Richard Cooper & Company of Portobello and Bonner & Company of the Barrowfield potteries manufactured much of the stoneware bottles, and J. & R. Tennent, with a view to cutting out the middleman, had their own pottery in Glasgow.

Hitherto, it was common for the wealthy to have a pin of ale in the cellar, but the problem was that if it was not all consumed within a week or so it went stale, and there was also the problem of waste due to sedimented yeast and hops. The advantages of switching to bottled beer meant that there was

no tapping or spiling and the beer remained fresh with a lively condition. Early bottled beer was, of course, bottled-conditioned, which meant that there was also a degree of wastage due to a small amount of yeast sediment. This did not go entirely to waste, however, as yeast was considered to be a health tonic containing the important B vitamins, and therefore it was considered to be a good dietary supplement. It was also considered to be beneficial for one's complexion, a cure for boils and constipation!

When glass bottles became more popular each bottle was free-blown individually, which meant that production was slow, but by 1810 bottles were made by blowing molten glass into a wooden hinged mould, which left a seam down the edge. The bottle top was moulded separately and then stuck on and its seam was always 90° to the bottle seam. In 1823, Henry Ricketts invented a bottle-moulding machine by air blowing the molten glass into several chilled cast-iron moulds. However, a major setback in the development in mass production was the introduction of the glass tax imposed in 1746, but after the tax was abolished in 1845 glass became cheaper and bottled beer started to gain popularity. By the 1860s, Tennent's had become the leading exporter of bottled beer in the world.

It is often claimed that nineteenth-century brewers avoided bottling in clear glass because they understood the adverse effects that light had on the beer producing skunky aromas. This is not so, however, and it was simply that the glass tax was higher on clear glass, which attracted more revenue from the many windows of large houses, and accordingly it was also dubbed the Window Tax. Consequently, many gable-ended windows were removed and bricked up and fake windows painted on in their place to reduce the tax burden; hence a saying we have today about daylight robbery! Brewers, and others such as chemists, coloured their bottles brown or green to avoid the hated tax.

Today it is recognised that brown glass in particular cuts down on the adverse effects that daylight has on beer, called 'light struck 'or 'sun struck', which produces skunky aromas. Basically, what happens is that at a certain wavelength the light cleaves off a side chain of the α-acid molecule that it then combines with sulphur-containing compounds, and this new molecule is responsible for the pong! The abolition of the glass tax was also responsible for the switch from pewter tankards to glass vessels so that the customer could see that he was getting a clear beer and full measure.

To avoid imitations and fraudulent practices that were very common with exported beers, brewers embossed their bottles with either their name or that of the brewery. Of course, this also gave them free advertising, and with the help of a ½*d* deposit ensured that the empty bottle was returned to the original source. Also, to ensure that tampering was avoided, the bottle stopper was sealed with a neck strap, which is a paper strip glued over the screw top and down on both sides of the neck of the bottle, and should be unbroken at the time of purchase. By the 1870s bottle manufacture became seamless, and this suited the practice of machine labelling, although dual embossing and labelling remained in vogue well into the twentieth century.

The standard bottle sizes were the quart, which was often used for popular porter, the pint, the half-pint and the nip, the latter being a bottle of 6fl oz (170ml) that were reserved for strong ales. The early bottles were filled by gravity and sealed with a cork, which was forced into the neck of the bottle by a leather

'flogger', and then wired in position to stop the cork flying out under the natural pressure built up by the bottle conditioning. Finally, the corks were sealed with coloured wax. Eventually bottles were filled by siphon fillers, and by the 1870s primitive bottling machines were becoming common.

The early glass beer bottles were designed with a bold shoulder that was considered necessary for bottle conditioned beer, so that when it was being decanted into the glass the yeast dregs were caught inside the shoulder that had now become a sump. This, of course, was not universal and there are ample examples of bottles closed with a swing stopper and screw top designed with a sloping shoulder.

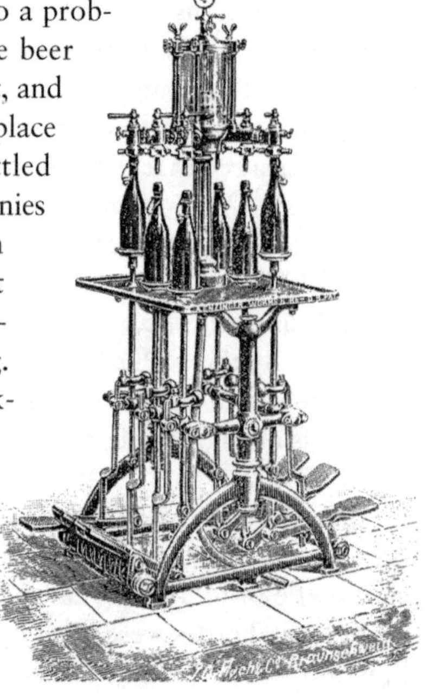

Exporting beer was also a problem, as in many cases the beer would continue to ferment, and as the cork was wired in place the bottle exploded. Bottled beer for export to the colonies was carefully packed with straw and stored upright in casks, and the cask re-headed to prevent pilfering. Many of the bottle breakages and casks that had blown out their shives resulted in a great loss of beer, and this was put down to the conditions at sea. However, as the clipper ships also carried thousands of emigrants to the colonies, many of the losses were a result of theft by thirsty travellers! Casks were particularly prone to theft as the bungs could be removed and the contents syphoned off and replaced with seawater. Another problem for the exporters was the ubiquitous ship's rat that could gnaw through casks for a quick one!

Scottish brewers exporting beer for the army contracts shipped in hogsheads to be bottled at the destination. This practice was more economical due to the cheap labour in the colonies, and cut down on the weight and cost of transporting glass and stone.

By the 1880s, technology had moved on, and J. & R. Tennent of Wellpark had installed a most ingenious machine that could automatically fill, cork and wire 5,000 bottles per day. Cork remained the principal bottle stopper material until 1875, when the American Charles de Quillfeldt invented the 'swing stopper' that became very popular on the continent. Scottish ale brewers such as Ballingall's of Dundee also used the swing stopper for their pale ales, and Jeffrey's and J. & R. Tennent preferred the swing stopper for their lager beer. In 1880, Henry Barrett invented the internal screw stopper, which became the main type of beer bottle close in Scotland until the 1960s, as it was more suitable for automatic bottling machines. A 'screw top' was a popular description for a pint bottle of pale ale regardless of who brewed it. The swing stopper and the screw top were popular as the bottle could be resealed if not all of the contents were consumed in one go.

Many brewers were quick to spot the growth of bottled beer and acquired an interest in bottle manufacture. In Dundee, Provost William Lindsay, who was a corn merchant and partner in the Brewing Company of Lower Pleasance (Later Ballingall's), had a share in a bottle-making works in the area of the docks. To meet with increasing demand for bottled beer, George Younger of Alloa built an enlarged bottling plant in

1889 known as the Kelliebank Bottling Department (latterly known as the Scottish Central Glass Works). The Kelliebank Bottling Department is said to have been the first of its kind in Scotland, producing the first generation of carbonated 'sparkling' beers, and such was the demand for bright bottled beer that Archibald Arrol, of Alloa, had a large bottling plant at 119 East Milton Street, Glasgow.

In 1892, the American William Painter invented the Crown Cap, a most ingenious device that sealed the bottle by crimping the cap onto the rim of the bottle. This type of closure, however, did not completely replace the screw stopper until the 1960s.

By the turn of the twentieth century, Scottish brewers employed three methods of bottling: (1) Strong ales should be racked just above the final gravity into a suitable sealed vessel and allowed to mature. As such beers will eventually be quite clear at bottling time, this necessitates the need to prime them with 'Gyle-wort' (Krausen wort'), which is actively fermenting wort that will bring the beer in bottle into condition. (2) The brew is rested until it only displays a degree of opalescence, which indicates that sufficient yeast remains in suspension to act upon the priming sugar. Alternatively, the beer may be fined and bottled before it drops bright. The beer is now primed and brought into rapid condition by storing it at a relatively high temperature and chilled before serving. (3) The beer is racked into a sealed container and primed and allowed to

condition under pressure. Before bottling, the brew is chilled to retain the dissolved CO_2, and it is carefully bottled so as not to lose any significant amount of gas. Alternatively, the beer may be racked clean of yeast, chilled to between 1and 2°C and top CO_2 pressure applied at 0.3 Bar for several days. The top pressure is applied as long as the beer accepts the gas and a pressure gauge is recommended. Prior to bottling the container is slowly vented, but the beer must remain chilled throughout the bottling to retain the CO_2.

In 1903, Geo. Younger of Alloa installed the most up-to-date bottling plant, which could automatically wash the bottles, chill and carbonate the beer and fill 1,000 bottles per hour! To continue to meet the demand for bottled beers, Younger's acquired the former Eglinton Dye Works and reconstructed it into the Export Bottling Plant. McLennan & Urquhart of the Dalkeith Brewery advertised on their labels that the brew was naturally conditioned but free from sediment, and obviously such brews were conditioned in bulk prior to bottling and not bottle conditioned.

After filling, the bottles were passed through jets of water to ensure that they were spotlessly clean, and finally 'sighted' by human eye – usually by young women who were used for cheap labour– to look for any bottles not correctly filled, or specks of dirt before passing through the labelling machine. It was also very important to check that no rogue bottles belonging to another brewer had found their way into the bottling hall.

After 1918, the public taste had moved on from the traditional heavy sweet beers towards lighter ales and bottled beers, and Wm. Younger installed the latest chilling and carbonating plant at Milton House in 1920, which formed part of the Holyrood Brewery. The first beer to be bottled was 90/- Sparkling Ale, which was first brewed in the late nineteenth century, at 1,200 pint screw-stopper bottles per hour and half-pints at 1,800 bottles per hour! The new and lighter ale called

'Holyrood Sparkling Ale' was also bottled in half-pints at the same rate. In the 1930s, Wm. Younger's beers were bottled under the watchful eye of bottling manager Frank Alexander. With the demand for bright bottled beer now established, John Jeffrey of Edinburgh also installed the latest chilling and carbonating bottling plant for his popular lager beer. By the 1930s, bottle design had changed to a gradual sloping shoulder that suited the majority of bright beers on the market. Today we see a return of the bold shoulder design although very few beers are bottled conditioned.

In 1930, James Aitken of the Falkirk Brewery had installed a chilling and carbonating plant for pale ale and lager, with bottles supplied by the Alloa Glass Company, and so the trend continued and by the end of the decade the majority of breweries in Scotland had taken up with the new bottling technology. The smaller local breweries had their beers bottled for them by specialist bottlers or larger breweries.

When technology became available for bright artificially conditioned sediment-free beer, sales of bottled beer increased, and by the turn of the twentieth century accounted for 5 per cent of the total UK market. Before the outbreak of the Second World War, sales peaked at 25 per cent, and by the mid 1950s had reached 35 per cent. At this time, it was estimated that some 2,500,000,000 bottles of beer were produced in the UK, which averaged fifty bottles per head of the population, which represented just over six gallons out of a total of eighteen gallons per person per annum.

In the 1930s, McEwan's were early pioneers in container beer that stayed fresh for up to a year. In 1936, the first Scottish

canned beer arrived, brewed by Tennent's, and these cone-topped cans, similar to Brasso tins. McEwan's Red Label Sparkling Beer, Steel and Coulson's Scotch Ale, and Younger's of Alloa Husky Export quickly followed, and by the late 1950s canned beer had become well established. Originally, canned beer was only available in half pints (10fl oz) with the export market increasing to 12fl oz.

In the 1950s, Younger's were sending hogsheads of beers to their bottling plant at Kendal, Yorkshire, where 5,000 pints and 7,000 half-pints were bottled per hour, producing 500,000 bottles per week. The popularity of bottled beer declined in the late 1960s when keg beer took over the top spot. Canned beer was the natural successor to bottled beer and offered the same advantages of being bright, lively and fresh, with the added advantage that did not suffer from being 'lightstruck'. It was the Americans who led the way in 1935 with flat-topped cans that required a 'Church key', which is a metal piercer that hooks under the rim of the can and when levered upwards forces the sharp point into the top of the can, thereby creating an opening, and this was done on both sides to allow an easy flow.

In 1952, Wright's of Perth acquired Thompson, Craik & Co. Ltd, bottlers and aerated water manufacturers, and bottled Bass and Worthington naturally conditioned beers plus Barclay Perkins Red Label Stout.

In 1956, Tennent's introduced the 16 fl oz can, quickly followed by Younger's of Alloa for Treble Top Ale. In 1964, the ring-pull opener, which completely removed the throwaway aluminium tab, was introduced. However, convenient as this was, it led to a problem of litter, and so the industry produced a ring-pull that remained firmly attached to the can after opening. Eventually the industry settled on the 16 fl oz can (454ml). It was also inevitable that larger cans would come on the market, with a 4-pint option available, and today 5-litre volumes are popular.

Beer cans also became a cheap place for advertising, and during the 1960s Tennent's Piper Export, which was described as, 'The most satisfying Export,' displayed a piper from the Scottish regiments. From 1965 to 1991, Tennent's lager opted for the popular Lager Lovelies, displaying provocative photographs of female models. This later fell out of favour when such advertising was considered inappropriate, but by this time the Lager Lovelies had probably run their course. At this time Scottish humour produced a joke about musical bars selling Piper Export, Harp lager and a fiddler behind the bar!

In the 1970s, Tennent's installed the Steinecker Brewhouse System at Wellpark that could produce up to nine brews per day, which was sufficient to fill almost 2 million bottles of lager. Tennent's also installed one of the fastest canning lines in Europe, which was capable of filling cans at a speed of 5,000 cans an hour.

The next stage in canned beer was the introduction in the 1990s of the so-called 'widget', which was patented by Guinness for 'draught' in a can. When the can was opened the widget released a surge of 70 per cent nitrogen and 30 per cent CO_2 and the whole contents of the can were continuously poured into a pint glass, producing a cloudy-looking pint that slowly cleared as the mixed gasses separated from the beer to leave a soft beer with a tight creamy head.

ENDNOTES

1. Alexander, John. *A Guide to Craft Brewing*. The Crowood Press, 2006.
2. Alexander, John. *Brewing Lager*. The Amateur Winemaker & Home Brewer, 1986.
3. Alexander, John. *Dundee Breweries*. 2008.
4. Alexander, John. *Scots Style*. The Amateur Winemaker & Home Brewer. 1985.
5. Alexander, John. *Shilling Ales*. The Amateur Winemaker & Home Brewer. 1983.
6. Alexander, John. *Shilling Ales*. Brewer's Contact, 2008.
7. Bain, Robert. *The Clans and Tartans of Scotland*. Collins, London, 1968.
8. Barnard, Alfred. *Noted Breweries of Great Britain and Ireland*. Four volumes.
9. Berry, C. J. J. *First Steps in Winemaking*. Amateur Winemaker Publications Ltd, 1980.
10. Berry, C. J. J. *Home Brewed Beers and Stouts*. AW Publications Ltd, Andover, 1970.
11. Black, Wm. *A practical treatise on brewing, and on storing of beer*. Smith, Elder & Co. Cornhill, London, 1835.
12. Blyth, Danny and Susan Oaks. *Low Alcohol. A report by CAMRA on low alcohol lagers and beers*. Campaign for Real Ale, 1988.
13. Brewery History Society. *Century of British Brewers, 1890–2004*.
14. Burt, Edmund. *Burt's Letter from the North of Scotland*. Birlinn Ltd, 1998.
15. Cornell, Martin. *Beer; The Story of the Pint*. Headline Publishing, London, 2003.
16. Corran, H. S. *A History of Brewing*. David & Charles, London, 1975.
17. Craig, Mair. *History of the Incorporation of Coopers of Glasgow*. Neil Wilson Publishing Ltd, 2004.
18. Dallas, John and Charles McMaster. *The Beer Drinker's Companion*. The Edinburgh Publishing Company Ltd, 1993.
19. Devine. T. M. *The Scottish Nation*. Penguin Books, 1999.
20. Donnachie, Ian. *A History of the Brewing in Scotland*. John Donald Publishers, 1979.
21. Duffus, Innes, Archivist, the Nine Incorporated Trades of Dundee. *Historical Records of the Guild Court Records & Maltmen Fraternity*.
22. *Dundee Advertiser*, 1896.

23.Dunn, Michael. *The Penguin Guide to Real Draught Beer*. Penguin Books, 1979.
24.Fraser, Jean. *Traditional Scottish Dyes*. Canongate Publishing, Edinburgh, 1996.
25.Glover, Brian. *Brewing for Victory*. The Lutterworth Press, 1995.
26.Hammond. Nicholas. *Wild Flowers*. The Wildlife Trust, 2002.
27.Harrison, Dr John. *Old British Beers and How to Brew Them*. Durden Park Beer Circle, 1991 & 2003.
28. Hind, H. Lloyd. *Brewing Science and Practice*, Volumes 1 & 2. Chapman & Hall, London, 1943.
29. Hornsey, Ian. *A History of Beer and Brewing*. RSC Publication, 2003.
30.Hughes, David. *'A Bottle of Guinness please'*. Phimboy, Woking, Berkshire, 2006.
31.Hunter, Sandy. Monkscroft, Belhaven, Dunbar.
32.Jeffery, E. J. *Brewing, Theory & Practice*. Nicholas & Kay, London, 1956.
33.*Journal of the Brewery History Society*, number 124/5.
34.Keir, David. *The Younger Centuries*. McLagan & Cumming Ltd, 1951.
35.Kenna, Rudolph and Anthony Mooney. *Peoples Palaces, Victorian and Edwardian Pubs of Scotland*. Paul Harris Publishing, Edinburgh, 1983.
36.King, Frank A. *Beer Has a History*. Hutcheson's Scientific & Technical Publications, 1947.
37.Lockhart, Wallace. *The Scot and his Oats*. Luath Press, Edinburgh, 1983.
38.McMaster, Charles. *Alloa Ale*. Alloa Brewing Company Ltd, 1985.
39.McMaster, Charles. Personal communication.
40.McMaster, Charles. *Edwin Scrimgeour and the Prohibitionist Party*. SBA Newsletter, No. 17, 1990.
41.McMaster et al. *Real Ale in and Around Edinburgh*. CAMRA Scotland, 1986.
42.McMaster et al. *The Wee Murray*. The Charmed Circle of Edinburgh, January 1983. Dundee Public Libraries Local Collection.
43.McNeill, Marion. *The Scots Cellar*. Lochar Publishing, 1992.
44.Molyneux, William. *Burton-on-Trent, Its Waters and its Breweries*. 1869. Reproduced by David Dover, Loughborough.
45.Newsom, Wilf. *Hey, Mr. Porter*! The Amateur Winemaker & Home Brewer, 1980.
46.Noonan, Gregory. *Scotch Ale*. Brewer's Publications, Boulder, Colorado, USA, 1993.
47.Owen, Colin C. 'The Greatest Brewery in the World'. *A History of Bass, Ratcliff & Gretton*. Derbyshire Record Society, 1992.
48.Parker, Hubert H. *The Hop Industry*. P.S. King & Son Ltd, London, 1934.
49.Pattinson, Tom. Translation of *History of the Spaten Brewery*. 1997.
50.Protz, Roger. *Pulling a Fast One*. Pluto Press, 1978.
51.Protz, Roger. *300 Beers to try before you die*. Campaign for Real Ale, 2005.
52.Readers Digest Nature Lovers Library. *Trees and Shrubs of Britain*. 1981.
53.Readers Digest Nature Lovers Library. *Wild Flowers of Britain*. 1981.
54.Reports of the Board of Customs and Excise (HMSO). 1938–43.
55.Roberts, W. H. *The Scottish Ale Brewer*. A & C Black, Edinburgh, 1847.

56.Southby, E. R. *A Systematic Handbook of Practical Brewing*. The Brewing Trade Review, 1895.
57.Southgate, D. G. *Edwin Scrimgeour*. Dundee Abertay Historical Society Publication No. 13, 1968.
58.Steel, James. *Selection of the Practical Points of Malting and Brewing and Strictures Thereon, for the use of Brewery Proprietors*. Robert Anderson, 22 Ann Street, Glasgow, 1878.
59.Sykes, Dr Walter. *The Principles and Practices of Brewing*. Charles Griffin and Company Ltd, London, 1897.
60.The Bass Museum, Burton upon Trent.
61.The Scottish Brewing Archive.
62.Thornhill. Martin. *Explorers Scotland*. Skefferton & Son, 1952.
63.Warrack, Alexander. *The Scots Dialect Dictionary*. Lomond Books, 1911. New Orchar Editions, 1988.
64.Wright & Coy (Perth) Ltd. Sandeman Public Library, Perth.

PICTURE CREDITS

Page No.

4. Frontispiece, Bell's Local History Library, Perth.
11. Pictish stone, courtesy of the National Museums of Scotland, Chambers Street, Edinburgh.
30. Tartan Special Chequebook, the author's collection.
40. Hawkhill Brewers Old Bally, the authors collection.
49. Hops, courtesy of the James Hutton Institute, Invergowrie, Perthshire.
56. Seed fiddle, Simon McMillan, BA Hons.
68. Drying barley, Keith Robson, DA.
70. The strae kiln, Keith Robson, DA.
86. Plans for Ballingall's New Park Brewery, 1875. Courtesy of Historic Environment Scotland, Edinburgh.
90. The open cooler at the Half Moon Brewery, Bruges. Authors collection.
101. The Cromdale Bar, Hawkhill. Dundee. Courtesy of Local History Library, Dundee City Council.
107. Courtesy of the Labologists Society.
109. The Prohibitionist, courtesy of the Local History Library, Dundee City Council.
115. The Unions in Wm. Younger's Abby Brewery. From Noted Breweries of Great Britain and Ireland, by Alfred Barnard, Causton and Sons, London, 1889-90.
117. Steels masher, from the Principles and Practice of Brewing, Walter Sykes, Charles Griffin & Co. 1897.
120. The sacharometer, the author's collection.
121. The sparger, from the Principles and Practice of Brewing, Walter Sykes, Charles Griffin & Co. 1897.
123. Trickle cooler at the Half Moon Brewery, Bruges. Author's collection.
127. Shilling Ales. Edinburgh branch of CAMRA local real ale guide, early 1980's.
134. The Labologists Society.
141. The home of the Menestheus. Bell's Local History Library. Perth.
144. The Labologists Society.
169. The Labologists Society.
188. Porter vats. Simon McMillan BA Hons.
195. The Labologists Society.

204 Water engine sketch, from The Wee Murray, McMaster et al, 1980's.

207. Tall founts, Duncan McAra, Scottish Tall Founts Supporters.
209. Dalex tall fount. Author's collection.
214. Early 19th century bottling apparatus. The Amateur Winemaker and Home Brewer, 1984.